Discard

D1226473

JIMI HENDRIX
STARTING AT ZERO

His Own Story

JIMI HENDRIX

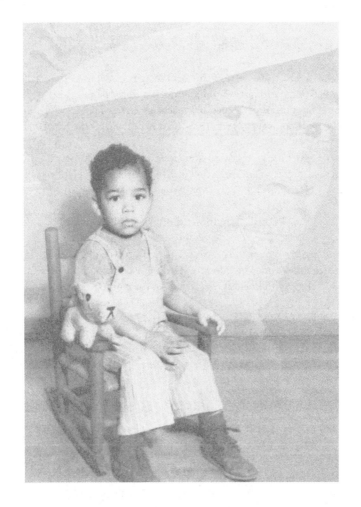

STARTING AT ZERO

BLOOMSBURY

NEW YORK · LONDON · NEW DELHI · SYDNEY

Starting At Zero (originally titled *Room Full Of Mirrors*) was produced without the input, assistance, or authorization of Al Hendrix, Janie Hendrix, Experience Hendrix, L.L.C., or any parties associated therewith.

Published by Bloomsbury USA, New York

All papers used by Bloomsbury USA are natural, recyclable products made from wood grown in well-managed forests. The manufacturing processes conform to the environmental regulations of the country of origin.

LIBRARY OF CONGRESS CATALOGING-IN-PUBLICATION DATA HAS BEEN APPLIED FOR.

ISBN: 978-1-62040-331-0

First U.S. Edition 2013

1 3 5 7 9 10 8 6 4 2

Typeset by Wherefore Art?
Printed in the United States of America by RR Donnelley, Willard, Ohio

CONTENTS

INTRODUCTION

To all intents and purposes this book has been written by Jimi Hendrix. But since it has been compiled posthumously, it seems only fair to offer an explanation as to how the final text was arrived at.

In a way, even the idea for the book came from Jimi himself. It evolved out of a film biography of him I was working on with Alan Douglas. Not wishing to put words into Jimi's mouth, we began experimenting with dialogue culled from records of things he had actually said. An enormous dossier was compiled from all sources that could be definitively authenticated. There was a superabundance of material, since during his four years in the spotlight, he was constantly giving interviews. He was also a compulsive writer, using hotel stationery, scraps of paper, cigarette cartons, napkins – anything that came to hand.

Although extracts from some of these interviews and writings have been published before, they have all too often been commandeered to support other people's ideas about his life and music. Yet on reading through all the available material, it is clear that Jimi left behind his own remarkable and comprehensive account of himself, albeit in a fragmented and somewhat elliptical manner. We felt it imperative that, amongst the plethora of myths and half-truths, Jimi should be allowed to offer his own personal version of his life and music.

Starting At Zero is the result of reorganizing this material into a narrative order. As a filmmaker, it seemed only natural to go about the task as if I were editing documentary film footage. The fact that Jimi's speech patterns are so rhythmic and his turns of phrase so visually rich served to enhance this approach. In a remarkable and haunting way, the book took on a life of its own. It began to develop of its own free will, so much so that I began to wonder, if this is "ghost writing," exactly which one of us is the ghost?

In saying that, I suppose what I'm really doing is paying tribute to the extraordinary power of Jimi's presence through his words.

In fact, he told his story so well that I had to take very few liberties. Apart from eliminating repetitions, I have very occasionally combined sentences or changed grammar where it seemed necessary to clarify the meaning. Also, because the source material was not originally intended to be used in this way, I have added brief notes to give essential background information and assist the continuity of events. Lyrics are included not simply because they are referred to in the text, but also because the body of Jimi's songs are in themselves autobiographical. He always claimed that for him, life and music were inseparable. In the absence of his music, which is the one true testimony, they constitute an essential poetic dimension.

Jimi's memories of the first twenty-three years of his life fell easily into a narrative order. For obvious reasons he never gave a clear and consecutive account of the last four years. He did, however, speak at length of the ideas that were forming in his mind and of the changes of perception and consciousness he was experiencing. Accordingly, as the book progresses, it becomes less an account of external events and more an exploration of an internal journey. This internal journey is the crux of the book – most appropriately, since the crossing of boundaries is at the heart of Jimi's story.

Up to some point the working title for this book was *Letter To A Room Full Of Mirrors*. The mirror was an image Jimi became obsessed with during the last years of his life. It can be seen as a symbol – or the threshold of the most important crossing of all. According to Native American traditions, the mirror of self-reflection represents our normal state of humanity, a state of self-imprisonment in which we view the world from a conditioned, repetitive and therefore non-creative standpoint. In these terms, to break the mirror of self-reflection means to reach beyond this limited world view to the infinite possibilities of the creative source itself.

> *Such a one's vision, ideas and inspirations come pristine from the primary springs of human life and thought. Hence they are eloquent, not of the present, disintegrating society and psyche, but of the unquenched source through which society is reborn. The hero has died as a modern man; but as eternal man – perfected, unspecific, universal man – he has been reborn.* [JOSEPH CAMPBELL]

If this book works at all, it is because Jimi was willing to speak about himself with such sensitivity, candor and humor. In this respect we must give special thanks to the many journalists who interviewed Jimi and to the collectors who recorded and preserved the material from which the book has been compiled. I would particularly like to thank Michael Fairchild for his tireless efforts in locating and authenticating the source material and also for his boundless enthusiasm and creative input; Christopher Mould for his invaluable support and participation during the difficult period of the genesis of the book; and Kevin Stein for his patience and sensitivity in helping me to finalize the last draft. Finally, I am eternally grateful to Alan Douglas for giving me the opportunity to work on such a deeply rewarding project. His knowledge and advice have throughout provided invaluable guidelines, and it is his foresight and dedication that have made it possible to produce this book.

PETER NEAL

I USED TO LIVE IN A ROOM FULL OF MIRRORS

ALL I COULD SEE WAS ME
WELL, I TAKE MY SPIRIT AND CRASH MY MIRRORS
NOW THE WHOLE WORLD IS HERE FOR ME TO SEE
I SAID, THE WHOLE WORLD IS HERE FOR ME TO SEE
NOW I'M SEARCHING FOR MY LOVE TO BE

BROKEN GLASS WAS ALL IN MY BRAIN
CUT, 'N SCREAMIN', CRYIN' IN MY HEAD
BROKEN GLASS WAS ALL IN MY BRAIN
IT USED TO FALL OUT OF MY DREAMS AND CUT ME IN MY BED
IT USED TO FALL OUT OF MY DREAMS AND CUT ME IN MY BED
I SAID, MAKING LOVE WAS STRANGE IN MY BED

LOVE COME SHINE OVER THE MOUNTAIN
LOVE COME SHINE OVER THE SEA
LOVE COME SHINE ON MY BABY
THEN I'LL KNOW EXACTLY WHO'S FOR ME
LORD, I'LL KNOW WHO I'LL BE FOR ME

I USED TO LIVE IN A ROOM FULL OF MIRRORS

ALL I COULD SEE WAS ME
WELL I TAKE MY SPIRIT AND CRASH MY MIRRORS
NOW THE WHOLE WORLD IS HERE FOR ME TO SEE
I SAID, THE WHOLE WORLD IS HERE FOR ME TO SEE
NOW I'M SEARCHING FOR MY LOVE TO BE

BROKEN GLASS WAS ALL IN MY BRAIN
CUT'N SCREAMIN', CRYIN' IN MY HEAD
BROKEN GLASS WAS ALL IN MY BRAIN
IT USED TO FALL OUT OF MY DREAMS AND CUT ME IN MY BED
IT USED TO FALL OUT OF MY DREAMS AND CUT ME IN MY BED
I SAID, MAKING LOVE WAS STRANGE IN MY BED

LOVE COME SHINE OVER THE MOUNTAIN
LOVE COME SHINE OVER THE SEA
LOVE COME SHINE ON MY BABY
THEN I'LL KNOW EXACTLY WHO'S FOR ME
LORD, I'LL KNOW WHO'LL BE FOR ME

CHAPTER ONE
(November 1942–July 1962)

VOODOO
CHILD

WELL, THE NIGHT I WAS BORN
LORD, I SWEAR THE MOON TURNED A FIRE RED.
WELL, MY POOR MOTHER CRIED OUT
"LORD, THE GYPSY WAS RIGHT"
AND I SEE'D HER FELL DOWN RIGHT DEAD …

I was born in Seattle,
Washington,
USA,

on November 27th,
1942

at the age of ZERO.

I REMEMBER A NURSE PUTTING A DIAPER ON ME and almost sticking me. I must have been in the hospital sick about something, because I remember I didn't feel so good. Then she took me out of this crib and held me up to the window, and she was showing me something up against the sky. It was fireworks — so it must have been the Fourth of July. That nurse turned me on, being high on penicillin she probably gave me, and I was looking up and the sky was just . . .

S s s c h u u s s s S c h u s h
Our first trip there!

I also remember when I was small enough to fit into a clothes basket. And I remember when I was only four and I wet my pants, and I stayed out in the rain for hours so I would get wet all over and my mom wouldn't know. She knew though.

Dad was very strict and levelheaded, but my mother used to like dressing up and having a good time. She used to drink a lot and didn't take care of herself, but she was a groovy mother. There were family troubles between my mother and father. They used to break up all the time, and my brother and I used to go to different homes. I stayed mostly at my aunt's and grandmother's. I always had to be ready to go tippy-toeing off to Canada.

My grandmother's Indian. She's part Cherokee. There's a lot of people in Seattle that have Indian mixed in them. It's just another part of our family, that's all.

I used to spend a lot of time on her reservation in Vancouver, British Columbia. There's a lot of them on the reservation, man, and it was really terrible. Every single house is the same, and it's not even a house, it's like a hut. It's just a really bad scene. Half of them are down on skid row, drinking and really completely out of their minds. And they're not doing anything. I used to get so mad that I just . . . just didn't pay too much attention when the teacher told us that Indians are bad! I mean, in other words, "All Indians are bad because they've got the clap!"

Now my grandma lives in a groovy apartment building in Vancouver. She has a television and a radio and stuff like that. She still has her long silvery hair though.

When I was little she used to tell me beautiful Indian stories, and the kids at school would laugh when I wore the shawls and poncho things she made. You know, the regular sob story. She gave me a little Mexican jacket with tassels. It was real good, and I wore it to school every day in spite of what people might have thought, just because I liked it. I liked to be different.

[AL AND LUCILLE HENDRIX DIVORCED IN DECEMBER OF 1950. JIMMY AND HIS YOUNGER BROTHER LEON REMAINED WITH THEIR FATHER. JIMMY SAW HIS MOTHER FOR THE LAST TIME IN JANUARY OF 1958. SHE DIED THE FOLLOWING MONTH.]

There's a dream I had when I was real little about my mother being carried away on these camels. It was a big caravan, and you could see the shadows of the leaf patterns across her face. You know how the sun shines through a tree? Well, these were green and yellow shadows. And she was saying to me, "Well, I won't be seeing you too much anymore, you know, so I'll see you."

About two years after that she died. I always will remember that one. I never did forget. There's some dreams you NEVER forget.

*   *   *   *   *   *   *

MOSTLY MY DAD TOOK CARE OF ME. He was religious, and I used to go to Sunday school. He taught me that I must respect my elders always. I couldn't speak unless I was spoken to first by grown-ups. So I've always been very quiet. But I saw a lot of things. A fish wouldn't get into trouble if he kept his mouth shut.

My dad was a gardener, and he'd once been an electrician. We weren't too rich! It got pretty bad in the winter when there wasn't any grass to cut. He used to cut my hair like a skinned chicken, and all my friends used to call me "Slick Bean."

I used to be really lonely. I'd bring a stray dog home every night till my pa let me keep one. Then it was the ugliest of them all. It was really "Prince Hendrix," but we just called it dawg! I used to have cats too. I love animals. Deer and horses are the prettiest. I used to see a lot of deer around Seattle. One time I saw this deer, and something went through me for one second, like I'd seen him before. I mean it was like I had some real close connection with that deer for one split second. I said, "Wait!" and then it just went away.

I went to school in Seattle, then Vancouver, British Columbia, where my folks came from. Then back to Seattle, at Garfield High School. On the whole my school was pretty relaxed. We had Chinese, Japanese, Puerto Ricans, Filipinos . . . We won all the football games!

At school I used to write poetry a lot, and then I was really happy. My poems were mostly about flowers and nature and people wearing robes. I wanted to be an actor or a painter. I particularly liked to paint scenes on other planets – *Summer Afternoon On Venus,* and stuff like that.

The idea of space travel excited me more than anything. The teacher used to say, "Paint three scenes," and I'd do abstract stuff, like *Martian Sunset*, no bull!

She'd say, "How are you feeling?"

and I'd say something kind of spacey like,

"Well, that depends on how the people on Mars are feeling."

I just didn't know what else to say to her.

I got tired of saying, "Fine, thank you."

She told me, "Well, you go to the front for that." So I'd go into the little cubbyhole, just like the Gestapo motorcycles – the driver sits on the motorcycle and the commander sits in the cubbyhole. I never could sit with everybody else. My teacher sat next to me in the third grade and said, "Now this is an example!" and at the same time she was touching my kneecaps under the table.

They said I used to be late all the time, but I was getting A's and B's. The real reason was I had a girlfriend in the art class, and we used to hold hands all the time. The art teacher didn't dig that at all. She was very prejudiced.

She said, "Mr. Hendrix, I'll see you in the cloakroom in three seconds please." In the cloakroom she said, "What do you mean talking to that white woman like that?" I said, "What are you, jealous?" She started crying, and I got thrown out. I cry easy.

[JIMMY DROPPED OUT OF GARFIELD HIGH SCHOOL IN OCTOBER 1960, AT THE AGE OF SEVENTEEN.]

I REMEMBER WHEN
    THEY THREW ME GENTLY OUT OF SCHOOL.
        THEY SAID I DON'T MEAN NO GOOD ...
    AND I FELT SO PROUD THAT I SCREAMED
    SO LOUD, "GO TO HELL,
        OUT OF STYLE SCHOOL!"

    YOU WAIT & WAIT, STILL NOTHING
    COMES TO SAVE YOU FROM THIS
        BORING FATE OF LIVING LIKE AN ANGEL.
YOU'RE ALWAYS DOING RIGHT, NEVER HAVE
    TO FIGHT, NEVER GET AN APPETITE
        FOR TAKING YOUR FIRST STEP
AROUND THE CORNER.

I left school early. School was nothing for me. I wanted something to happen to me. My father told me to look for a job. So that's what I did for a couple of weeks. I worked for my father. I had to work very hard. We had to carry stones and cement all day, and he pocketed the money. He didn't pay me. He just kept all the money for himself. I didn't want to work so hard for so little money, so I started bumming around with the kids.

Sometimes, with a couple of friends we'd hit a cop, and we'd have a helluva fight a half hour later. Sometimes you'd end up in jail, but you'd eat very well. Most of the cops were bloody bastards, but there were also some very good ones. They were more personal – they wouldn't hit you so hard, and you could eat better then. But it all got very boring after a while.

Lots of kids have it tough. Jesus! I couldn't stand it at home. I ran away a couple of times because I was so miserable. Once I ran away after a blazing row with my dad. He hit me in the face, and I ran away. When my dad found out I'd gone he went pretty mad with worry. But then I didn't really care about other people's feelings. I came home when I realized my dad was upset. Not that I cared but, well, he is my dad. I don't think my dad ever thought I was going to make it. I was the kid who didn't do the right thing.

TEARS BURNING ME
 TEARS BURNING ME IN MY EYES
 WAY DOWN, WAY DOWN IN MY SOUL.
 TEARS BURNING ME IN MY SOUL . . .

 WELL, I GOTTA LEAVE THIS TOWN
 GONNA BE A VOODOO CHILE
 AND TRY TO BE A MAGIC BOY.
 COME BACK AND BUY THIS TOWN
 COME BACK AND BUY THIS TOWN
 AND PUT IT ALL IN MY SHOE
 MIGHT EVEN GIVE A PIECE TO YOU!

When I was upstairs at home the grown-ups had parties, listening to Muddy Waters, Elmore James, Howlin' Wolf and Ray Charles. That sound was really not evil, just a thick sound. I'd sneak down after and eat potato chips and smoke butts. The Grand Ol' Opry used to come on, and I used to watch that. They used to have some heavy cats, heavy guitar players.

The first guitarist I was aware of was Muddy Waters. I heard one of his records when I was a little boy, and it scared me to death because I heard all those sounds. Wow! What was all that about? It was great. I liked Muddy Waters when he had only two guitars, harmonica and bass drum. Things like *Rollin' And Tumblin'* were what I liked – that real primitive guitar sound.

My dad danced and played the spoons. My first instrument was a harmonica, which I got when I was about four, I suppose. Next it was a violin. I always dug string instruments and pianos, but I wanted something I could take home or anywhere, and I couldn't take home a piano.

Then I started digging guitars. Everybody's house you went into seemed to have one lying around. One night my dad's friend was stoned, and he sold me his guitar for five dollars. I didn't know that I would have to put the strings 'round the other way because I was left-handed, but it just didn't feel right. I can remember thinking to myself, "There's something wrong here."

I changed the strings 'round, but it was way out of tune when I'd finished. I didn't know a thing about tuning, so I went down to the store and ran my fingers across the strings on a guitar they had there. After that I was able to tune my own.

I was about fourteen or fifteen when I started playing guitar. I played in my backyard at home, and kids used to gather 'round and said it was cool. Then I got tired of the guitar and put it aside. But when I heard Chuck Berry it revived my interest.

I learned all the riffs I could. I never had any lessons. I learned guitar from records and the radio. I loved my music, man. I'd go out to the back porch there in Seattle, because I didn't want to stay in the house all the time, and I'd play guitar to a Muddy Waters record. You see, I wasn't ever interested in any other things, just the music. I was trying to play like Chuck Berry and Muddy Waters. Trying to learn everything and anything.

WHEN I WAS SEVENTEEN I FORMED THIS GROUP with some other guys, but they drowned me out. I didn't know why at first, but after about three months I realized I'd have to get an electric guitar. My first was a Danelectro, which my dad bought for me. Must have busted him for a long time. But I had to show him I could play first. In those days I just liked rock and roll, I guess. We used to play stuff by people like the Coasters. Anyway, you all had to do the same things before you could join a band. You even had to do the same steps. I started looking around for places to play. I remember my first gig was at an armory, a National Guard place, and we earned thirty-five cents apiece and three hamburgers.

It was so hard for me at first. I knew about three songs, and when it was time for us to play onstage I was all shaky, so I had to play behind the curtains. I just couldn't get up in front. And then you get so very discouraged. You hear different bands playing around you, and the guitar player always seems like he's so much better than you are.

Most people give up at this point, but it's best not to. Just keep on, just keep on. Sometimes you are going to be so frustrated you'll hate the guitar, but all of this is just a part of learning. If you stick with it you're going to be rewarded. If you're very stubborn you can make it.

I used to see the numbers one, nine, six, six in my dreams. I had very strange feelings that I was here for something and I was going to get a chance to be heard. I got the guitar together because that was all I had. **Oh Daddy, one of these days I'm gonna be big and famous. I'm gonna make it, man!**

A LITTLE BOY INSIDE A DREAM
JUST THE OTHER DAY
HIS MIND FELL OUT OF HIS FACE
AND THE WIND BLEW IT AWAY.
A HAND CAME OUT FROM HEAVEN
AND PINNED A BADGE ON HIS CHEST
AND SAID, GET OUT THERE, MAN, AND DO YOUR BEST.

*   *   *   *   *   *   *

{In May 1961, Jimmy was arrested for riding in a stolen car.
He was given a two-year suspended sentence after the public defender
told the judge that Jimmy was going to enlist in the armed forces.}

Jimmy to the judge:

"Yes, Sir.
I've been thinking about being
a Screaming Eagle."

I was eighteen. I didn't have a cent in my pocket. I'd just spent seven days in the cooler for taking a ride in a stolen car, though I never knew it was stolen. I figured I'd have go in the army sooner or later, so I walked into the first recruiting office I saw and volunteered. I was thinking about playing then. I was slightly playing. I knew about four songs on the guitar. You know, the usual rumble. I wanted to get everything over with before I tried to get into music as a career, so they wouldn't call me up in the middle of something that might be happening.

I had no musical training, so I couldn't sign up as a musician. I figured I might as well go all the way, so I joined the airborne. I did it because I was bored, but the army taught me what boredom is. There's nothing more monotonous than spending a whole day peeling potatoes.

I hated the army immediately.

{SOME TIME AFTER LUCILLE'S DEATH, A FRIEND OF AL'S, WILLENE, MOVED INTO THE HENDRIX HOUSEHOLD, TOGETHER WITH HER DAUGHTER, WILLETTE.}

LETTER HOME, JUNE 1961:

Dear Mr & Mrs James A. Hendrix,

Well, I know it's about time for me to write. We had a lot of things to do down here though. How's everybody up there? Fine, I really hope. The weather here is pretty nice except that it's pretty windy at times because the ocean is only about 2 miles away. I can't say too much because we have to clean the barrack up a little before we go to bed. I just wanted to let you know that I'm still alive, although not by very much. All, I mean all, my hair's cut off and I have to shave. I've only shaved two times so far counting tonight since I've been here. I won't be able to see you until about 2 months from now — that's if I'm lucky. We're going through Basic training, that's the reason. Although I've been here for about a week, it seems like about a month. Time passes pretty slow even though we do have a lot to do. How's the gardening business? I hope it's doing fine. I believe it's more expensive being in the army than living as a civilian. So far we had to get two laundry bags $1 each, a block hat $1.75, two locks 80 cents each, 3 towels 50 cents each, stamping kit $1.75, haircut $1, shoe polish kit $1.70, shaving razor, blades and lather $1.70, insignias 50 cents. So I guess this isn't all that good financially, as I first thought . . .

We don't get paid until June 30th 1961, so I would like to know if you can send me 5 or 6 dollars. They only gave us $5.00 when we first came and all that's gone except $1.50 and that isn't going to last a minute around here. I can and will pay you back at the end of this month when we get paid if you could send it. After we get situated things will be way better. It's just this first mixed-up month that messes us up. So I really must close now. Please, if you have time, write back and tell me what's going on up there.
Give everybody my love – Grandma, Gracie, Willie May, Uncle Frank, Betty, etc., etc.

From James, with love.
p.s. Please if you can send a few dollars as soon as you can
— thank you.

The training was really tough. It was the worst thing I've ever been through. They were always trying to see how much you could take. There was one thing we used to call the "hanging agony." You would be left hanging in a harness on a rope with your feet just a few inches from the ground. You'd be like that an hour some days, and if the harness was slightly in the wrong position it was hell. And they only gave you about three seconds to put the harness on. They tried to make us tough – so we had to sleep in the mud. The whole idea was to see how much you could take. I took it. I was determined not to crack.

LETTER HOME, OCTOBER 1961:

Dear Dad,

I just received your letter and I'm so glad to hear that you're doing OK and that Leon and you are together. That took me by surprise and I really am so happy about that, because I know it does, or should I say it did, get lonesome around there by yourself. That is the way I feel when I start thinking about you and the rest – and Betty. Tell Leon to do what he's supposed to because, just as you used to tell me, it pays off later in life. I'm so happy too about you getting a TV, and I know that you're fixing the house up "tuff." Keep up the good work and I'll try my very best to make this AIRBORNE for the sake of our name. I'm going to try hard and will put as much effort into this as I can. I'll fix it so the whole family of Hendrix's will have the right to wear the Screaming Eagle patch of the US Army Airborne (smile)! Take it easy and when you see me again I'll be wearing the patch of proudness. I hope.

To Daddy Hendrix from from your son, love James
p.s. Please send my guitar as soon as you can – I really need it now – it's still over at Betty's house.

FROM ANOTHER LETTER HOME:

There's nothing but physical training and harassment here for two weeks. Then when you go to jump school, that's when you get hell! They work you to DEATH! Fussing and fighting everything you do. You have to do 10, 15 or 25 pushups – pushing Tennessee around all day with my hands – exercising in wet sawdust in

temperatures six degrees below zero. They really make the sparks fly,
and then half the people quit. That's how they separate the men from
the boys. I pray that I will make it on the men's side.

I had to buy two pairs of jump boots and four sets of tailored
fatigues, plus twenty Screamin' Eagle patches. You know what that
represents? The 101st AIRBORNE DIVISION, Fort Campbell,
Kentucky — yes, indeedy!

LETTER HOME, NOVEMBER 1961:

Well, here I am, exactly where I wanted to be, in the 101st
Airborne. We jumped out of a 34-foot tower on the third day we were
here. It was almost fun. We were the first nine out of about 150 in
our group. When I was walking up the stairs to the top of the tower,
I was walking nice and slow, just taking it easy. There were three
guys who quit when they got to the top of the tower. They took one
look outside and just quit. You can quit any time. And that got me
thinking as I was walking up those steps, but I made up my mind
that whatever happens I'm not quitting on my own.

When I got to the top, the jump master snapped these two straps
onto my harness and slapped me on the butt and said right in my ear
"Go, Go, GO!" I hesitated for a split second, and the next thing I
knew, I was falling. All of a sudden, when all the slack was taken
up on the line, I was snapped like a bullwhip and started bounding
down the cable . . . While I was sliding down I had my legs
together, hands on the reserve, my chin tucked into my chest. I ran
smack dab into a sand dune. Later they'll show us how to go over it
by lifting our feet, of course. But my back was to it. Oh well, it was
a new experience.

love James

That was about the best thing in the army – the parachute drops. I did about twenty-five. It's the most thrilling thing I ever did before. It's just as much fun as it looks, if you can keep your eyes open.

When you first jump it's really outasight. Like you're in the plane, and some cats just NEVER been in a plane before. Some people were throwing up in a big bucket, you know, a big garbage can sitting in the middle.

It was great!

And then the plane was goin'

RRROOOAAARRRR!!! Just roarin' and shakin' and you can see the rivets just jumpin' around.

Talk about what am I doing here?

You're just there at the door and all of a sudden,

flop!
rush!

For a split second a thought went through me like,
"You're crazy!"

Physically it was a falling over backwards feeling,
like in your dreams.

And it's almost like blanking,
and it's almost like crying, and you want to laugh.

It's so personal, because once you get there
everything is so quiet.

All you hear is the breeze – ssssshhhhhhh – like that.

It's the most alone feeling in the world.

You're there all by yourself,
and you can talk very low or you can scream or do anything.
And then I thought how crazy I was for doing this thing,

but I loved it anyway.

Then you feel that tug on your collar, and you're
supposed to look up and see if your chute is open. Every time
you jump you're scared that maybe this time it won't open.

And so you look up, and there's that
big, beautiful,
white mushroom above you.

That's when you begin talking to yourself again,
and you just say,

"Thank the Lord."

But the army's really a bad scene. I was stationed in Kentucky. Kentucky's right on the border of North and South, and in that camp were some of the orneriest, most boot-licking guys. Some of the officers, man! It was terrible! They wouldn't let me have anything to do with music. They tell you what you are interested in, and you don't have any choice. The army is more for people who like to be told what to do.

I was in for fifteen months, but I got injured on a jump and hung up on the discipline. One day I got my ankle caught in the skyhook just as I was going to jump, and I broke it. I told them I'd hurt my back too. Every time they examined me I groaned, so they finally believed me.

I was lucky to get out when I did, with Vietnam coming up.

CHAPTER TWO
(July 1962–September 1966)

HIGHWAY CHILE

HIS GUITAR SLUNG ACROSS HIS BACK,
HIS DUSTY BOOTS IS HIS CADILLAC.
FLAMIN' HAIR JUST A-BLOWIN' IN THE WIND,
AIN'T SEEN A BED IN SO LONG IT'S A SIN.
HE LEFT HOME WHEN HE WAS SEVENTEEN,
THE REST OF THE WORLD
HE HAD LONGED TO SEE,
AND EVERYBODY KNOWS THE BOSS
A ROLLIN' STONE GATHERS NO MOSS.
NOW, YOU PROBABLY CALL HIM A TRAMP,
BUT IT GOES A LITTLE DEEPER THAN THAT,
HE'S A HIGHWAY CHILE.

WALK ON, BROTHER.
DON'T LET NO ONE STOP YOU!

ONE MORNING I found myself standing outside the gate of Fort Campbell on the Tennessee-Kentucky border with my little duffel bag and three or four hundred dollars in my pocket. I was going back to Seattle, which was a long way away. But there was this girl I was kinda hung up on.

So I thought I'd have a look in at Clarksville, which was near, stay the night and go home the next morning. I went to this jazz joint and had a drink. I liked it and stayed. People tell me I get foolish good-natured sometimes. Anyway, I guess I felt real benevolent that day. I must have been handing out bills to anyone who asked me. I came out with sixteen dollars left! And it takes more than that to get from Tennessee to Seattle, because it's two thousand miles. So no going home!

I first thought I'd call long distance and ask my father to send some money, but I could guess what he'd say if I told him I'd lost nearly four hundred dollars in just one day. Nope. That was out. In the army I'd started to play guitar very seriously, so I thought all I can do is try to earn money playing guitar. Then I remembered that just before I left the army I'd sold my guitar to a cat in the unit. So I went back to Fort Campbell, found the guy and told him I just had to borrow the guitar back.

IT TOOK ME SOME TIME to get better from the injuries I had, and then I went down South. I played in cafes, clubs and on the streets. It was pretty tough at first. I lived in very miserable circumstances. I slept where I could, and when I needed to eat I had to steal it. I earned some money, but I didn't like it at all. Then I started a group called the King Kasuals with a fellow called Billy Cox who played funky, funky bass.

In Clarksville we worked for a setup called W & W. Man, they paid us so little that we decided the two W's stood for "Wicked and Wrong." This one-horse music agency used to come up on stage in the middle of a number, slip the money for the gig into our pockets and disappear. By the time the number was over and I got a chance to look in the envelope, I'd find they'd only slipped us a couple of dollars instead of ten or fifteen.

Then we got in with a club owner who seemed to like us a lot. He bought us some new gear. I had a Silvertone amp, and the others got Fender Bandmasters. But this guy took our money, and he was sort of holding us back. So I moved about some more.

I went to Nashville, where I lived in a big housing estate they were building. They hadn't put the floor in yet and there were no roofs, so we had to sleep under the stars. That was wild.

Every Sunday afternoon we used to go downtown to watch the race riots. You were supposed to call up some of your friends and say,

"We're going to be shoutin' at you down there tonight, so be there."

We'd take a picnic basket because they wouldn't serve us in the restaurants. One group would stand on one side of the street and the rest on the other side. They'd shout names and talk about each other's mothers and every once in a while stab each other. That would go on for a couple of hours, and then we'd all go to some club and get stoned. Sometimes, if there was a good movie on that Sunday, there wouldn't be any race riots.

I used to have a childhood ambition to stand on my own feet, without being afraid to get hit in the face if I went into a "white" restaurant and ordered a "white" steak. But normally I just didn't think along these lines. I had more important things to do — like playing guitar.

In Nashville I played all kinds of stuff, even some rockabilly. In Nashville everybody knows how to play guitar. You walk down the street, and people are sitting on the porch playing more guitar . . .

That's where I learned to play, really.

WHEN I FIRST STARTED PLAYING GUITAR it was way up in Seattle, and they don't have too many of the real blues singers up there. When I went down South, all the cats there were playing blues, and that is when I really began to get interested in the scene. I just listened to the way people played blues guitar, and I dug it.

I adore "folk blues." "Blues" to me means Elmore James, Howlin' Wolf, Muddy Waters and Robert Johnson. I like Robert Johnson. He's so cool. That sort of music gets the message over and comes through so easily. It doesn't necessarily mean that "folk blues" is the only type of blues in the world. You can have your own blues. Everyone has some kind of blues to offer, you know.

In Atlanta and Georgia there are some great guys, like Albert King and Albert Collins. Albert King plays completely and strictly in one way – just straight funk blues, new blues guitar, very young, funky sound – which is great. One of the funkiest I've heard. He plays strictly that way, so that's his scene.

Most of the guitarists come from the South. Down South at some funky club one cat there starving to death might be the best guitar player you ever heard, and you might not even know his name.

NASHVILLE USED TO BE A FUNNY SCENE, with all those slick managers trying to sign up hillbilly singers who'd never been in a big town before. It was like a game, like one big put-on all the way. Everybody trying to take everyone else. But once you knew how to watch out for yourself it could be a lot of laughs.

I met a guy called Gorgeous George in Nashville, and he got me on some tours. So I started traveling around, playing around the South. It was one of the hardest audiences. Guys must play really good because for these people you can't play less. They'll recognize this. They hear it all the time. We played in bars on top of the platform, and it was really hot and the fans wanted more and more. Cats used to jump on the guitar, and there used to be cats playing behind their heads or playing with their teeth or elbows. Sometimes they'd switch instruments, just for fun.

Some cat tried to get me to play behind my head because I never would move around too much. I said, "Oh, man, who wants to do all that junk?" And then, all of a sudden, you'd start to get bored with yourself, because those people were really hard to please. The idea of playing guitar with my teeth came to me in a town in Tennessee. Down there you have to play with your teeth or else you get shot! There's a trail of broken teeth all over the stage.

After that I traveled all over the States, playing in different groups. Oh God, I can't remember all their names. I used to join a group and quit them so fast! There I was, playing in this Top 40 R&B Soul Hit Parade Package, with the patent leather shoes and hairdo combined.

But when you're running around starving on the road, you'll play almost anything. I got so tired of feeding back on *The Midnight Hour*. I didn't hear any guitar players doing anything new, and I was bored out of my mind.

I learned how not to get an R&B band together. The trouble was too many leaders didn't seem to want to pay anybody. Guys would get fired in the middle of the highway because they were talking too loud on the bus or the leader owed them too much money – something like that. Bad pay, lousy living, and gettin' burned – that was those days.

I STAYED IN BUFFALO for about a month or two, but it was too cold up there. Seattle has a different type of cold. It's a nice coldness, not so cutting as Buffalo. Anyway, there's this girl up there trying to work "roots" on me, trying to work this Voodoo stuff, keep me there, you know? There's different things they can do. They can put something in your food or put some little hair in your shoe. She put a lock of hair in the heel of my shoe. Crazy cat! But she must have tried it half-heartedly, because I was only sick in the hospital for two or three days.

You wouldn't think this sort of thing happens till it happens to you. But I can tell you it's real scary when it does. Around the southern states they have scenes like that. I saw it. If I see it happen or if I feel it happen, then I believe it. A person gives off certain electric shocks anyway, so if the vibrations are strong enough to get these charms working, they can actually do it.

THEN I WENT TO NEW YORK and won first place in the Apollo amateur contest, you know, twenty-five dollars. I dig playing at the Apollo Theater. So I stayed up there, starved up there for two or three weeks. I'd get a gig once every twelfth of never. I lived in very miserable circumstances. Sleeping among the garbage cans between them tall tenements was hell. Rats runnin' all across your chest, cockroaches stealin' your last candy bar from your very pockets. I even tried to eat orange peel and tomato paste.

People would say, "If you don't get a job you'll just starve to death." But I didn't want to take a job outside music. I tried a few, including car delivery, but I always quit after a week or two. I'd worry a bit about not having any money but not enough to go out and rob a bank.

Then one of the Isley Brothers heard me playing in a club and said he had a job open. So I played with the Isley Brothers for a while, and they used to make me do my thing (play with my teeth, etc.), because it made them more bucks or something. Most groups I was with didn't let me do my own thing.

But it wasn't so groovy after all. I had to sleep in the clubs where they were playing, and there were a lot of cockroaches and rats. The bastard animals were all over you during the night! I quit the Isley Brothers in Nashville. I got tired of playing in the key of F all the time, so I turned in my white mohair silk suit and patent leather shoes and began playing on the street corners again.

After a couple of months there was a soul package coming into town with Sam Cooke, Solomon Burke, Jackie Wilson, Hank Ballard, B.B. King and Chuck Jackson, and I got a little job playing in the backup band. I learned an awful lot of guitar picking behind all those names every night.

Then I got stranded in Kansas City, Missouri, because I missed the bus and didn't have any money. This group came up and brought me back to Atlanta, Georgia, where I met Little Richard. I had to do an audition with him and he liked me, so I started playing with him for a while. But I got the feeling that I couldn't really develop under his influence.

He wouldn't let me wear frilly shirts on stage. Once, me and Glen Willings got fancy shirts because we were tired of wearing the uniform. After the show Little Richard said,

"Brothers, we've got to have a meeting.
I am Little Richard.
`I am the King of Rock 'n' Rhythm`
and I'm the only one who's going to look pretty on stage.
Glen and Jimmy, will you please turn in those shirts
 or else you will have to suffer the consequences of a fine."

He had another meeting over my hairstyle. I said I wasn't going to cut my hair for nobody.
"That'll be a five dollar fine for you."
If our shoelaces were two different types we'd get fined five dollars. Everybody on the tour was brainwashed.

I guess I played with Little Richard for about five or six months. I worked with him all over America, finally landing in Los Angeles where I had enough of Richard. I quit because of a money misunderstanding. He didn't pay us for five and a half weeks. You can't live on promises when you're on the road, so I had to cut that mess loose.

I WENT BACK TO NEW YORK and played with this little rhythm and blues group named Curtis Knight and the Squires. I made a few records and arranged a few songs for him. I also played with King Curtis and Joey Dee. I played Cleveland Arena with Joey Dee and the Starliters, in some rhythm and blues show that had Chubby Checker in it.

Mind you, I jumped from the frying pan into the fire when I joined with Joey Dee and the Starliters. This is an outasight group – but! Nobody talked to me. I was just another Negro guitarist. So after sucking on a "Peppermint Twist" salary I had to quit and began playing with a jukebox band. I finally quit that too.

I had nothing but a "wish sandwich" – two pieces of bread, wishing I had some meat between.

*   *   *   *   *   *   *

LETTER HOME FROM NEW YORK, AUGUST 1965:

*I just want to let you know I'm still here, trying to make it.
Although I don't eat every day, everything's going alright for me.
I still have my guitar and amp, and as long as I have that, no fool
can keep me from living.*

*There's a few record companies I visited that I probably can
record for. I think I'll start working toward that line because when
you're playing behind other people you're still not making a big name
for yourself, as you would if you were working for yourself. But I
went on the road with other people to get exposed to the public and see
how business is taken care of, and mainly just to see what's what.
After I put a record out, there'll be a few people who know me
already and who can help with the sale of the record. Nowadays
people don't want you to sing good. They want you to sing sloppy and
have a good beat to your songs. That's what angle I'm going to shoot
for. That's where the money is. So just in case about three or four
months from now you might hear a record by me which sounds
terrible, don't feel ashamed, just wait until the money rolls in,
because every day people are singing worse and worse on purpose and
the public buys more and more records.*

*It could be worse than this, but I'm going to keep hustling and
scuffling until I get things to happening like they're supposed to for
me. Tell everyone I said hello. Leon, Grandma, Ben, Ernie, Frank,
Mary, Barbara and so forth. Please write soon. It's pretty lonely out
here by myself. Best luck and happiness in the future.*

Love, your son Jimmy

I just got tired, man. I just couldn't stand it anymore. I can't tell you the number of times it hurt me to play the same notes, the same beat. I was just a kind of shadowy figure up there, out of sight of the real meaning. I wanted my own scene, making my own music. I always wanted a lot, you know? I really, really did. I was starting to see that you could create a whole new world with an electric guitar, because there isn't a sound like it in the whole world!

I had these ideas and sounds in my brain, but I needed people to do it with and they were hard to find. I had friends with me in Harlem, and I'd say, "C'mon down to the Village so we can get something together."

But they were lazy, they were scared, plus they didn't think they were going to get paid. I said, "Quite naturally you won't get paid on the audition, because it's us going down there and being aggressive, it's us filtering down to them. So there's a few things you have to give up in the beginning." They didn't want to do that, so I just went down to the Village and started playing like I wanted.

I N GREENWICH VILLAGE people were more friendly than in Harlem, where it's all cold and mean. I couldn't stand it there because they talk about you worse than anyplace else! When I was staying in Harlem my hair was really long, and sometimes I might tie it up or do something with it. I'd be walking down the street, and all of a sudden the cats, or girls, old ladies – anybody! – would be just peekin' out, sayin',

"Ough, what's this supposed to be? Black Jesus?"

or

"What is this, the circus or something?"

God! Even in your own section.

Your own people hurt you more.

The Village was groovy. I'd just lay around and play for about two dollars a night and then try to find a place to stay. You had to chat someone up real quick before you had a place to stay. I got a break playing guitar for John Hammond Jr. at the Cafe Au Go Go. That was great because the ceiling was really low and dusty. I'd stick the guitar right up into the ceiling. It was like war. You didn't even need a smoke bomb!

WHEN I WAS DOWN IN THE VILLAGE Bob Dylan was also starving down there. I saw him one time, but both of us were stoned out of our minds thanks to demon ale. It was at this place called the Kettle of Fish. I remember it vaguely. We were both stoned and just hung around laughing. Yeah, we just laughed.

When I first heard Dylan I thought, you must admire the guy for having that much nerve to sing so out of key. But then I started listening to the words. That sold me.

I used to get bored so quickly by anybody and everything. That's why I went towards Dylan, because he offered me something completely new. He used to have a pad with him all the time to put down what he saw around him. He doesn't have to be stoned when he writes, although he probably is. A cat like that just doesn't have to be. I could never write the kind of words he does, but he's helped me out in trying to write because I've got a thousand songs that will never be finished. I just lie around and write about two or three words, but now I have a little more confidence in trying to finish one.

POSTCARD TO AL HENDRIX, 1966:

Dear Dad.

Well ... I'm just dropping in a few words to let you know everything's so-so in this big raggedy city of New York. Everything's happening bad here. I hope everyone at home is alright. Tell Leon I said hello. I'll write you a letter real soon and will try to send you a decent picture. So until then I hope you're doing alright. Tell Ben and Ernie I play the blues like they NEVER heard.

Love always, Jimmy

The first real group I got together on my own was with Randy California. That would be around the beginning of 1966, I guess. I changed my name to Jimmy James and called the group the Blue Flames. Not exactly original, was it?

Almost immediately we got offers from Epic and CBS, but I didn't feel we were completely ready then. Record companies had started to show a little interest in me when I was playing at the Cafe Au Go Go, and a year before Mick Jagger had tried to get me on a tour. But my big slice of luck came when a little English friend persuaded Chas Chandler, the bass player of the Animals, to come down where we were gigging and give an ear.

The Animals were doing their last gig as a group in Central Park, you know, "mouth the words." Chas came down and heard me and asked would I like to come over to England and start a group there. He seemed like a pretty sincere guy, and I'd never been to England before.

I said, "I might as well go," because that's the way I live my life. I'd never been to Memphis, so I'd starve my way down there. I didn't have any roots in the States that would hang me up, and it doesn't matter which bit of the world I'm in as long as I'm living and putting things down. Plus, I thought I could play louder over there, I could really get myself together over there. There wouldn't be so many hang-ups as there were in America, you know, mental hang-ups and things like that. I was getting all uptight with the American scene. The country wasn't opening up the way England was.

I only hope that the guys I left behind are all right. We were making something near three dollars a night, and we were starving. The way I left was kinda wrong. They all thought they were going, but it was easier for me to go alone. I felt kind of rotten about leaving just like that because we weren't living too much, you dig?

I always had a feeling that, if my mind was right, I'd get a break someday. It took a long time, knocking around and playing a lot of dates that didn't pay very well, but I figure it was worth it. Oh, man! I don't think I could have stood another year of playing behind people.

I'm glad Chas rescued me.

CHAPTER THREE
(September 1966–June 1967)

ARE YOU EXPERIENCED?

I KNOW, I KNOW YOU'LL PROBABLY SCREAM
AND CRY
THAT YOUR LITTLE WORLD WON'T LET YOU GO.
BUT WHO IN YOUR MEASLY LITTLE WORLD
ARE YOU TRYING TO PROVE THAT
YOU'RE MADE OUT OF GOLD AND CAN'T BE SOLD.
SO, ARE YOU EXPERIENCED?
HAVE YOU EVER BEEN EXPERIENCED?
WELL, I HAVE.
LET ME PROVE IT TO YOU …

I'm in England, Dad.

I met some people, and they're going to make me a big star.

We changed my name to . . .

JIMI.

September 23, 1966. That's when I came to England. They kept me waiting at the airport for three or four hours because I didn't have a work permit. At one point there was talk of sending me back to New York until it was all sorted out. They carried on like I was going to make all the money in England and take it back to the States!

I moved into a flat with Chas Chandler. It used to belong to Ringo. In fact, they only took the drums away the other day. There's stereo all over the place and a very kinky bathroom with lots of mirrors. Immediately complaints started to pour in. We used to get complaints about loud, late parties when we were out of town! We'd come back next morning and hear all the complaints. Chas got real mad about it, but I didn't let it bug me.

THE FIRST TIME I PLAYED GUITAR in England I sat in with Cream. I like the way Eric Clapton plays. His solos sound just like Albert King. Eric is just too much. And Ginger Baker, he's like an octopus, man. He's a real natural drummer. When you see him working all you can see are arms and legs.

I couldn't work too much because I didn't have a permit. If I was going to stay in England I had to get enough jobs to have a long permit. So what we had to do was line up a lot of gigs. Chas knows lots of telephone numbers. He helped me find my bassist and drummer and form the Jimi Hendrix Experience. It was very hard to find the right sidemen, people who were feeling the same as me.

After a lot of tryouts we had a jam, and Noel Redding came 'round. He'd come to audition for the New Animals, and we happened to be in the same building. Noel likes nice gutsy rock and used to play lead guitar in a group named The Loving Kind. Chas asked him to try playing the bass, and I dug his hairstyle and it worked out perfect. Noel thinks lead when he plays bass. Almost every great bass player does that. I picked him because he could play ANYTHING on the bass.

Mitch Mitchell was the best we heard out of about twenty drummers. He used to play with Georgie Fame and the Blue Flames, and he'd just quit the group about two days before. He's more of a classic drummer, more of a funky R&B type drummer. Mitch is a jazz addict, and he keeps on about this cat Elvin Jones all the time. He played me a record once by Elvin Jones, and I said, "Damn, that's you!"

I was thinking of the smallest piece [group] possible with the hardest impact. If it had taken two or twenty or ten — but it came out as a trio, which is great. I figure that if you have a rhythm guitar player it's going to slow down the whole thing, because you have to show him exactly what you want. If you want to do something, it's best to do it yourself, right?

We did try the organ for about fifteen minutes, and it didn't work out. It made us sound like just anybody. With this trio lineup we are very flexible. We can still improvise quite a bit, which is lacking from too many other groups. If I'd had two blues men with me we would have gone straight into one bag, the blues, and that's not for me. I mean, I love the blues, but I wouldn't want to play it all night. There are some blues that just make me sick. I feel nothing from it. And we're not going in for any of this *Midnight Hour* kick.

No "Gotta, gotta, gotta,"

because we don't "have ta, have ta, have ta!"

We don't want to be classed in any category. My music isn't pop. It's ME. My guitar is my notes, our notes, regardless of where they came from.

We're trying to create our own personal sound, our own music and our own personal being. We are into our own personal history, what we are, until we have settled down inside of us.

It's a real foundation thing, like where you can imagine from.

It's very primitive thought, you know.

That's why I like us being called the EXPERIENCE.

It's right.

Four days after we got together we were playing at the Paris Olympia with Johnny Hallyday, who is like the French Elvis. We got together with *Midnight Hour, Land Of A Thousand Dances, Everyone Needs Someone To Love* and *Respect*. I adore the audience at Olympia, it's incredible. Paris Olympia is the biggest thing in Europe, and the kids there are like the kids at the Apollo in Harlem. I mean they really know what's going on. You know if you're no good you might die that night. That first time we played there they sat open-mouthed and didn't know how to accept us. But they still listened. That's one thing I really dug. It was beautiful.

When we get on stage we click, and I guess that's what really counts. Mitch and Noel are both excellent musicians in their own right, and they complement everything I do with taste and imagination. When we're jamming out there we try to listen to each other. We don't compromise with each other very much. Like one guy thinks one thing, and he's going to stick with that one thing. Sure, we don't always totally agree on what our music will do, but somehow we combine what we know best, somehow we make a song.

Part of the whole thing is seeing the reaction the group gets when we walk out onstage. We play really hard in the clubs. The club managers think we are an abomination, but the public thinks it's awesome. One time, we played at the new London club the Upper Cut where we had about five thousand turn up. It scared me half to death when I saw all those people out there! But I just went on and did what I felt like, and everything worked out all right.

At the Saville Theatre I had this gadget on the guitar that every time I hit a certain note the lights would go up. I would like to someday play a note and have it come out as a color with lights and film. That'll be the total experience!

The Beatles used to come and see us sometimes, like at the Saville Theatre, and Paul McCartney told me they were planning to do a film [*Magical Mystery Tour*], and he wanted us to be in this film. We weren't known then and McCartney was trying to help us, but we got a nice break before they got the movie together.

The Beatles and the Stones are all such beautiful cats off record, but it's a family thing, such a family thing, that sometimes it all begins to sound alike. Sometimes you don't want to be part of the family. I believe soon all the English records will sound alike, just like Motown all sound alike. That's nice in a way, but what happens if you have your own thing going?

POSTCARD TO AL HENDRIX, NOVEMBER 1966:

Dear Dad,

Well ... Although I lost the address, I feel I must write before I get too far away. We're in Munich, Germany, now. We just left Paris and Nancy, France. We're playing around London now. That's where I'm staying these days. I have my own group and will have a record out in about 2 months named 'Hey Joe'. By the Jimi Hendrix Experience. I hope you get this card. I'll write a decent letter. I think things are going a little better.

Your loving Son, Jimi.

{DECEMBER 16, 1966, FIRST SINGLE RELEASED IN THE U.K.}

We all dug *Hey Joe* as a number, so we put it down on record. While we were working on it I don't think we played it the same way twice. Lots of people have done different arrangements of it, and Timmy Rose was the first to do it slowly. I like it played slowly. There are probably 1,000 versions of it fast, by the Byrds, Standells, Love and others.

It was the first time I ever tried to sing on a record. I was too scared to sing. Chas made me sing serious. I just wish I could sing really nice, but I know I can't. I just feel the words out. I try all night to hit a pretty note, but I'm more like an entertainer and performer than a singer. Guitar is the basic thing for me. Voice is just another way of getting across what I'm doing musically.

{FEBRUARY 1967, *HEY JOE* REACHED #4 IN THE U.K. CHARTS.}

Hey Joe is really a blues arrangement of a cowboy song. It isn't quite a commercial song, so I'm surprised that it got so high in the hit parade. I'm just wondering how people are going to take the next one, because it's so different. They'd picked out *Love Or Confusion* to be our next single, but I had this thing on my mind about a dream I had that I was walking under the sea. It's linked to a story I read in a science fiction magazine about a purple death ray. It's called *Purple Haze* – excuse me!

PURPLE HAZE ALL IN MY BRAIN,
LATELY THINGS DON'T SEEM THE SAME,
ACTIN' FUNNY, BUT I DON'T KNOW WHY,
'SCUSE ME WHILE I KISS THE SKY.

PURPLE HAZE ALL AROUND,
DON'T KNOW IF I'M COMING UP OR DOWN.
AM I HAPPY OR IN MISERY?
WHATEVER IT IS, THAT GIRL PUT
A SPELL ON ME!

PURPLE HAZE ALL IN MY EYES,
DON'T KNOW IF IT'S DAY OR NIGHT.
YOU'VE GOT ME BLOWING, BLOWIN' MY MIND.
IS IT TOMORROW OR JUST THE END
OF TIME?

It's about this guy who doesn't know which way he's going. This girl turned this cat on, and he doesn't know if it's bad or good – that's all. It could be stuff like going into different strange areas like most curious people do. It's nothing to do with drugs. The key to the meaning of the song lies in the line *"that girl put a spell on me."* The song progresses from there.

We really had a funny time last night.
I met this girl and she was really outasight.
I said, baby, what you doin'?
She said, "Well, you know, I'm alright. How are you?"
I said, well, everything's the old thing, just a big drag.
I was just wonderin', what's that you got in that little sack there?
She said, "This?"
And she opened it up and it went like this ... {feedback}.

I said WHEW! Close it! Close it! Baby, look out!
She put her little thumb in. So I stuck my fingers in and

A big Purple Haze!"

{Released in March 1967, *Purple Haze* entered the U.K. charts in six days and reached #3.}

I would under no circumstances call my music psychedelic. We had guys ten years ago in the States playing what they're now calling psychedelic. You hear these cats saying, "Look at the band, they're playing psychedelic music," and all they're really doing is flashing lights on them and playing *Johnny B. Goode* with the wrong chords.

The ones who call themselves that are so bad. I'd hate to go on a trip and hear all that noise. Freak-out, psychedelic and so on, that's all pretty limited. I don't want anybody to stick a psychedelic label around my neck. Sooner Bach and Beethoven. Don't misunderstand me, I love Bach and Beethoven. I have many records by them, also by Gustav Mahler.

On the whole I think it's a mistake to try to divide different kinds of music into small categories. There really doesn't have to be any specific name for different kinds of music. The name of the band is good enough, isn't it? You might hear one little thing and say, "Hey, that's kind of nice," but our music's like that jar of candy over there. Everything's all mixed up. It's a mixture of rock, blues and jazz, a music that's still developing, that's just now coming, a music of the future. If it must be a tag, I'd like it to be called "Free Feeling." It's a mixture of rock, freak-out, blues and rave music. My rock-blues-funky-freaky sound.

I was influenced by everything at the same time – Muddy Waters, Jimmy Reed, Chet Atkins, B.B. King. I dug Howlin' Wolf and Elmore James, but I was into other stuff too – Ritchie Valens, Eddie Cochran and *Summertime Blues*. And you could also say that I was influenced by Bob Dylan and Brian Jones. I listen to everything, from

Bach to the Beatles. See, a mixture of those things, and hearing those things at the same time, which way do you go?

I was digging them for themselves, not for what I could get from them or wishing I could be like that. I'm not copying what I heard before. Like when you're a baby, you're used to one little thing, not using it but just used to it, sucking on it until you grow up, and then you don't think about it anymore. You've got to dig everything and then get your own ideas. Too much digging and not enough doing will set you spinning.

A LOT OF THE PEOPLE I listen to now are British. It's almost like being in the States! I don't believe they can sound exactly like the American cats, but a few do. Stevie Winwood and Spencer Davis come about the closest to really having that feeling. And Tom Jones! Why? I guess they get tired of hearing all those Herman's Hermits records. If they can really dig a cat like Ray Charles, who's one of the all-time greats when you're talking of soul, it isn't too surprising when they come up with that soulful feeling. It just shows that they're really listening.

*　　*　　*　　*　　*　　*　　*

You're a Sagittarian?

> Constantly. Twenty-seventh.

Personal points?

> 5 feet 11 inches; 11 stone 5 pounds; dark brown eyes – black
> sometimes; dark brown hair.

Origin of stage name?

> 88 percent from my birth certificate, 12 percent from
> misspelling.

Any pets?

> My two little furry-minded guitars.

Favorite food and drinks?

> Spaghetti, strawberry shortcake with whipped cream and
> banana cream pie. I like typical soul food too – greens and rice.

English food?

> Oh god! man. See, English food, it's difficult to explain.
> You get mashed potatoes with just about everything, and I
> ain't gonna say anything good about that!

What do you think of London?

> It's a different kind of atmosphere here. People are more
> mild-mannered. I like all the little streets and the boutiques.
> It's like a kind of fairyland. But you know what really turns
> me on about London? Just watching the girls go by. It's a
> fantastic city for girl-watchers. They're all so beautiful and so
> many different nationalities.

Do you smoke?

> If I didn't smoke I'd be fat as a pig. My nerves are very bad.
> I like tipped cigarettes mostly, alternating with menthol
> ones – about a pack over a day and a half.

Do you have any hobbies?

> I like to watch the lightning. Especially on the fields and
> flowers when I'm on my own. I read a lot of science fiction.
> And I love reading fairy tales, like Hans Christian Andersen,
> and *Winnie-the-Pooh*.

What don't you like?

> I don't like ordinary things or people with very neat eyebrows
> who look very neat.

What kind of person are you?

> I'm a little bit quiet, a little closed. Most of the time I don't
> talk so much. What I have to say I say with my guitar.

Immediate plans?

> I want to stay in England. In the States I was always playing
> behind other people, and I found it difficult to contain myself.
> It's much better now I have my own group. I understand
> there won't be any difficulty getting work permits and so on
> as long as I'm a good little boy.

How important is your music to you?

> For us it's very important. If we stop playing we have no
> money to buy food with.

Professional ambition?

> I want to be the first man to write about the blues scene
> on Venus.

Personal ambition?

> To see my mother and family again.

How long since you've been home?

> About seven years. I don't even know my six-year-old sister.
> I just called my dad once when I came to England to let him
> know I'd reached something.

What did he say?

> He asked me who I had robbed to get the money to go to
> England. Actually, I'm scared to go home. My father is a very
> strict man. He would straight away grab hold of me, tear my
> clothes off and cut my hair! I'd like to have enough money to
> send home to my father. One day I'm going to build him a
> house. Just to tease him a little bit, and because he paid for
> my first guitar.

Why do you wear your hair like that?

> I think maybe because my dad used to cut it all the time
> when I was a kid, and I used to go to school looking like a
> plucked chicken. Maybe that gave me a complex.

Do you comb your hair?

> No, I use a brush. A comb would get stuck. A girl asked me
> if she could comb my hair. NOBODY can comb my hair.

I can't even comb my hair. But I think this hairstyle is groovy. A mod Shirley Temple. A frizzy permanent. Anyway, it's better than having dull, straight hair. The strands, you see, are vibrations. If your hair is straight and pointing to the ground you don't get many vibrations. This way, though, I've got vibrations shooting out all ways.

Why is it necessary to be dressed peculiarly?

Well, I don't consider it actually necessary. This is the way I like to dress and look, off stage and on. I like shades of color that clash. I always wanted to be a cowboy, or Hadji Baba, or the Prisoner of Zenda. Before I go onstage my road manager says to me, "Jimi, you scruffy looking git, you're not going on looking like that tonight, are you?" And I say, "As soon as I've put out this cigarette – I'm fully dressed." I feel comfortable like this.

Where is fashion going?

I don't know, and I don't care, really. Maybe people will wear different colored sheets, like in the olden days. And don't ask me those silly questions about whether I wear underwear. I swear you should have gotten someone else for this interview.

PEOPLE ASK ME whether I dress and do my hair like this just for effect, but it's not true. This is me. I don't like to be misunderstood by anything or anybody, so if I want to wear a red bandanna and turquoise slacks and if I want hair down to my ankles, well, that's me. All those photographs you might have seen of me in a tuxedo and a bow tie playing in Wilson Pickett's backing group were me when I was shy, scared and afraid to be myself. I had my hair slicked back and my mind combed out.

The jacket I'm wearing now is Royal Army Veterinary Corps, 1898 I believe. Very good year for uniforms. The other night I was about half a block away from the Cromwellian Club, wearing this gear. Up comes this wagon with a blue light flashing, and about five or six policemen jump out at me. They look into my face real close and severe. Then one of them points to my jacket and says, "That's British, isn't it?" So I said, "Yeah, I think it is." And they frowned and all that bit, and they said, "You're not supposed to be wearing that. Men fought and died in that uniform." The guy's eyes were so bad he couldn't read the little print on the badges.

So I said, "What, in the Veterinary Corps? Anyway, I like uniforms. I wore one long enough in the United States Army." They said, "What? You trying to get smart with us? Show us your passport." So we did all that bit too. I had to convince them that my accent was really American. Then they asked me what group I was with, and I said the Experience. So they made fun of that as well and made cracks about roving minstrels. After they made a few more funnies and when they'd finally got their kicks, they said they didn't want to see me with the gear on anymore, and they let me go. Just as I was walking away one of them said, "Hey, you said you're with the Experience. What are you experiencing?" I said, "Harassment" and took off as quick as I could.

People take us strange ways, but I don't care how they take us. Man, we'll be moving, because in this life you've got to do what you want. You've got to let your mind and fancy flow, flow free.

WHITE COLLARED CONSERVATIVE FLASHING
DOWN THE STREET,
POINTING THEIR PLASTIC FINGER AT ME.
THEY'RE HOPING SOON MY KIND WILL DROP AND DIE,
BUT I'M GONNA WAVE MY FREAK FLAG HIGH, HIGH.
WOW! WAVE ON, WAVE ON.

FALL MOUNTAINS, JUST DON'T FALL ON ME.
GO AHEAD ON MR. BUSINESSMAN, YOU CAN'T DRESS LIKE ME.

Do you know my biggest problem? I just can't look straight into a camera and smile if I don't feel like smiling. I just can't do it. It's like being told to be happy to order! Anyway, the photographers always try to make me look so evil. All the photos I had done for publicity to begin with were picked because I looked so grim. We threw away all the smiley-smiley shots and kept the horrors. That made me a kind of monster. Honestly, I don't know why the people want to see me as a horror type. They'd love it if I'd look like a cannibal! But I guess it was necessary to get that visual thing going before we could make people listen.

{BY THE END OF MARCH 1967, THE HENDRIX EXPERIENCE HAD GIVEN OVER EIGHTY PERFORMANCES IN THE U.K., FRANCE AND HOLLAND. THE BRITISH TABLOIDS HAD DUBBED HENDRIX "THE WILD MAN OF POP."}

Some people ask what on earth am I? Are we being invaded? But the comments don't bother me. I used to listen to what people said, go away and lie in bed and worry about it. But you can't worry yourself about that. It's just conventional people wanting the whole world to be conventional with them. We set out to be a trip, that's the reason we are like this. We really want to freak them out when we play.

We play very, very loud. We play loud to create a certain effect, to make it all as physical as possible, so it goes right through you. It should hurt. We were in Holland doing a TV show, and the equipment was the best ever. They said play as loud as you like, and we were really grooving when this little fairy comes running in and yells, "Stop! Stop! The ceiling in the studio below is falling down!"

And it was too, plaster and all! I like to play loud. I always did like to play loud.

I get accused of being electrically hung up, but I like electric sounds, feedback and so forth. Static. People make sounds when they clap, so we make sounds back. Musically, "freak-out" is almost like playing wrong notes. It's playing the opposite notes to what you think the notes should be. If you hit it right, with the right amount of feedback, it can come up very nice. It's like playing the wrong notes seriously, dig? It's a lot of fun.

We don't use gimmicks for their own sake. What happens on stage is what I do myself. I mean, when I'm moving around out there I'm just squeezing that little bit more out of my guitar. Sometimes I jump on the guitar, sometimes I grind the strings up against the frets. The more it grinds, the more it whines. Sometimes I rub up against the amplifier, sometimes I sit on it, sometimes I play with my teeth, or I'll be playing along and I'll feel like playing with my elbow. I can't remember all the things I do. It's just the way I play. I'd die of boredom if I didn't put everything into it.

The one thing I really hate is miming. It's so phoney. I was asked to mime at a Radio London appearance, and I felt guilty just standing there holding a guitar. I can't feel the music when it's like that. You can't expect me to play guitar with my teeth when there is a recording going on in the background. That's crazy.

When you play with your teeth you have to know what you are doing or you might hurt yourself. Everywhere I go they tell me about one group who got up like us, and the fella tried to play the guitar with his teeth and his teeth fell out all over the stage. "That's what you get for not brushing your teeth," I tell them. I've never broken anything playing, but I was thinking once, for a freak-out of course, of putting bits of paper in my mouth before the show and then spitting them out like all my teeth were dropping out!

A LOT OF PEOPLE THINK what I do with my guitar is vulgar. I don't think it's vulgar. Perhaps it's sexy, but what music with a big beat isn't? Music is such a personal expression it's bound to project sex. What is so wrong about that? Is it so shameful? Is it any more shameful than some of the erotic adverts you see in the papers or on television? The world revolves around sex. Music should be matched with human emotions, and if you can tell me a more human one than sex, then you've got me fooled. Those who think we are filthy are the same people who don't want to let Joan Baez sing her anti-war songs publicly.

I play and move as I feel. It's not an act but a state of being. My music, my instrument, my sound, my body are all one action with my mind. It's like a contact high between the music and me. The actual music is like a fast, lingering high. It might be sex or love to certain people in the audience, but to me it just gets me stoned out of my mind. If they think our show is sexy, that's nice, and if the show gives them other feelings, that's just as good. If my music makes them feel free to do what they think best for themselves, that is a step ahead.

As long as they're not passive.

{MARCH 31, 1967, THE JIMI HENDRIX EXPERIENCE JOINED THE WALKER
BROTHERS' TOUR.}

The first night of the Walker Brothers' tour was when I started to worry. I knew where it was at when it came to specialist blues scenes, but this was in front of audiences who had come to see the Walker Brothers, Engelbert Humperdinck and Cat Stevens. All the sweet people follow us on the bill, so we have to make it hot for them. We have to hit 'em and hit 'em good.

Those who come to hear Engelbert sing *Release Me* may not dig me, but that's not tragic. You can only plan so far in these things. We'll play for ourselves. We've done it before, where the audience stands about with their mouths open, and you wait ten minutes before they clap.

I'm not trying to entertain the teenyboppers or the very old. I'm trying to be honest, and I'm trying to be me. I can't imagine the people buying Engelbert's discs are buying mine, unless they are musical freaks who buy every record because it's in the hit parade. I sat down and listened to Engelbert one night. He really has a very good voice. It's flawless. Maybe if you don't have a very good imagination you need good looks and a flawless voice.

*　　*　　*　　*　　*　　*

LETTER TO A FAN, APRIL 1967:

Dear David,

Stay groovy. I'm sorry to say that we don't have any more
photos of us at the moment. Some guys stole our whole supply
from the tour bus. But we all (all three of us) really
appreciate you writing us at this most crucial moment
(Walkers, Hump, Cat, everything against us).
Thanx again and the best of luck.

From Jimi Hendrix Experience.

THE TOUR BOSSES ARE GIVING US HELL. I don't know if it's like this on all tours, but they don't give us a chance to tune up before we go onstage. And just before I go on, I turn 'round and find a guitar string is broken, or I find my guitar is all out of tune after I just tuned it. I kinda don't know what to say about that. They just don't give a damn about us. They say we are obscene and vulgar. We refuse to change our act, and the result is my amplifier sometimes gets cut off at the funniest of times.

I have been threatened by the tour manager every night so far, but I'm not going to stop for him. I've been using this act all the way since I've been in Britain. There's nothing vulgar about it at all. I just don't know where these people get their ideas. But they are not getting rid of us unless we are officially thrown off the tour.

Naturally, there were some things we did for publicity. I mean, the flaming guitar thing I did was all rigged. We just poured petrol all over the damn thing and set a light to it. The security men went wild, but we made every paper! I remember the promoter, who was in on the trick, kept screaming at me and shaking his fist, shouting, "You can't do things like that, Hendrix! I'm having you off this tour!" Meantime he was concealing the evidence for me under his coat – my burned-up guitar that all the police and firemen were looking for.

THE TOUR WAS GOOD EXPERIENCE, but our billing position was all wrong. I was setting the stage on fire for everyone else. That Engelflumplefuff hadn't any stage presence. He never got anything going. Stopped it all stone dead. But it was a gas, in spite of the hassles.

I really learned a lot about British audiences, because every night we had two more to meet, and after each show Chas and I would discuss how everything went down and ways to improve. In the theater at Luton one guy jumped about twenty feet from a box onto the stage, just to shake hands with us. We'd step outside the stage door where the teenyboppers were and think, "Oh, they won't bother about us," and get torn apart! A girl was hanging on to my guitar saying, "You don't want it." I said to her, "You must be out of your mind!" We were good in something called Leicester too.

I feel embarrassed when I hear a compere giving me a big buildup before I go on stage or I see my name in lights outside a theater. I can't believe it's happening to me. Sometimes the audience says "Hooray" so loud it scares me out of my mind. I want to say, "Not so loud!" But I like it. It makes me feel like crying.

We three had a kinda feeling that we were on the way to success as far as Britain was concerned. Strange, because a lot of people don't know who we are individually. We would walk into a press conference as the three question marks and they would ask which one is which. I guess that emphasizes that it is what we have been playing which has got us off the ground.

{IN MAY 1967, SIX DAYS AFTER ITS RELEASE, *THE WIND CRIES MARY* ENTERED THE U.K. CHARTS. IT REMAINED THERE FOR ELEVEN WEEKS, REACHING A TOP POSITION OF #6.}

I don't know how it happened so suddenly, but our records began to sell at an incredible rate. *Purple Haze* is still in the charts right now. We never thought it would be this big. Maybe we should have waited for it to cool down before releasing *The Wind Cries Mary*. But in England you have to keep releasing records. They have very quick minds, and they get bored easily. They are very bizarre people in certain senses, which is exciting.

You can't blame me for being selfish by trying to get our songs across to the public as quick as possible. I really hate to lose out. If you're really interested and really involved in music, then you can be very hungry. The more you contribute, the more you want to make. It makes you hungrier, regardless of how many times you eat a day.

I JUST KEEP MUSIC IN MY HEAD. It doesn't even come out to the other guys until we go to the studio. That's what happened with *The Wind Cries Mary*. We were rehearsing on stage, and then it just came to me. The words came first, and the music was so easy to put there. The whole thing just melted together. It was recorded in about two takes.

I explained to Noel and Mitch what I had in mind, and we played it halfway through so that Chas could get the balance in the studio. Then we played it through once. Six minutes later the song was ready to be mastered and pressed. We never do more than five or six takes in a recording studio. It's too expensive!

When we cut a record we talk about a lot of things, except the music we have to record. We tell jokes, drink and smoke. Then we're in the right mood, and we start. That isn't easy. I like it better before an audience. I know how to play by the way they react, by the feeling with the audience. It gets me in the right mood. But you don't have that in the studio.

I believe I am more a musician than a songwriter. I only write my own songs because I don't want to do other people's. Chas helps me out with the lyrics on occasion. When I write a song he modifies a couple of words to make the lyrics come out better. I don't consider myself a songwriter, but I would love to be recognized as such.

Ever since Bob Dylan's been around people have been kicking him and saying, "Oh man, he sings like a broken-leg dog!" But they say that because they don't really understand his words. If people really want to dig him, they should go out and buy a book with his words in it and find out what he's saying. Everybody wants to know what happened to modern-day poetry. Well, you can find it all over the place. Just dig the records.

Dylan is giving me inspiration. Not that I want to sound like him – I just want to sound like Jimi Hendrix – but you have to write your own songs in order to get your own personal sound. Up to now I've written about one hundred songs, but most of them are in those New York hotel rooms I got thrown out of. I write a lot of words all over the place, on matchboxes or on napkins, anywhere. Sometimes the music comes across to me when I'm sitting around doing nothing, and then the music makes me think of a few words I might have written. So I go back to those few words, if I can find them.

Songs come from anywhere. You see everything, experience everything as you live. Even if you're living in a little room, you see a lot of things, and if you have imagination the songs just come. I spend a lot of time daydreaming. It's great to sit and dream. All kinds of nice thoughts pop up, songs too. I have to wait until they come to me, even if I've got a record date minutes away. I couldn't just keep on doing it for money constantly. I just want to turn people on and let them know what's happening. That's my reason for being around.

✷ ✷ ✷ ✷ ✷ ✷ ✷

THE ONLY WAY I CAN EXPLAIN MYSELF thoroughly is through songs. Most of the songs, like *Purple Haze* and *Wind Cries Mary* were about ten pages long, but then I had to break them all down. Maybe some of the meanings got lost by breaking them down, which is such a drag. The trouble is that a single has to be under six minutes. It used to be under three, which was a real hang-up. It's like you used to be able to give them just one page of a book. Now you can give them two or three pages, but never the whole book.

The Wind Cries Mary is a girl who has slightly taken to talking about me to her friends. One moment she will talk about me like a dog, and the next moment she says the complete opposite. But she is a nice girl underneath. It's nothing but a story about a breakup, just a girl and a boy breaking up, that's all. Like the traffic lights turning blue tomorrow. That means feeling bad in your mind. There's no hidden meaning. It's just a slow song, that's what I call it.

Slow, quiet.

AFTER ALL THE JACKS ARE IN THEIR BOXES
                AND THE CLOWNS HAVE ALL GONE TO BED
        YOU CAN HEAR HAPPINESS
                STAGGERING ON DOWN THE STREET
        FOOTPRINTS DRESSED IN RED
                AND THE WIND WHISPERS MARY

A BROOM IS DREARILY SWEEPING
                UP THE BROKEN PIECES OF YESTERDAY'S LIFE
SOMEWHERE A QUEEN IS WEEPING
SOMEWHERE A KING HAS NO WIFE
        AND THE WIND IT CRIES MARY

THE TRAFFIC LIGHTS THEY TURN BLUE TOMORROW
AND SHINE THEIR EMPTINESS DOWN ON MY BED
        THE TINY ISLAND SAGS DOWNSTREAM
        'CAUSE THE LIFE THEY LIVED IS DEAD
        AND THE WIND SCREAMS MARY

WILL THE WIND EVER REMEMBER
THE NAMES IT HAS BLOWN IN THE PAST
AND WITH ITS CRUTCH, ITS OLD AGE AND ITS WISDOM
        IT WHISPERS, "NO, THIS WILL BE THE LAST"
        AND THE WIND CRIES MARY

In music, you've got to say something real just as quick as you can. That's the idea of it, make it very basic. I don't mean my lyrics to be clever. I just say what I feel and let them fight over it, if it's interesting enough. What I want is for people to listen to the music and the words, as one thing. Maybe a lyric has only five words, and the music takes care of the rest. Instead of saying, "Will you make love to me tonight?" all of a sudden there's this big crash. You can make the sound happen.

You can put in a certain little freaky thing, like the sound of raindrops reversed and echoed and phased and all that, to emphasize a certain point. If the lyrics lose out completely to the music, or the other way 'round, then it's not done right. In the end, there has to be a complete marriage between the words and music.

{MAY 12, 1967, THE FIRST EXPERIENCE ALBUM WAS RELEASED IN THE U.K.}

We're calling our first album
Are You Experienced?

There's nothing wrong with that!

First off, I don't want people to get the idea it's a collection of "freak-out" material. This is a very personal album, just like all our singles. I guess you could call it an ad lib album because we did so much of it on the spot.

It's a collection of free-feeling and imagination. I've written songs for teenyboppers like *Can You See Me*, and blues things. There are only two songs that would give you the horrors if you were on a trip – *Are You Experienced?* and *May This Be Love*. But they are actually peace-of-mind songs. They are just relaxing things, like meditational shades. As long as you can get your mind together while you're listening to them, they've made it with you.

IF YOU CAN JUST GET YOUR MIND TOGETHER,
THEN COME ON ACROSS TO ME,
WE'LL HOLD HANDS AND THEN WE'LL WATCH THE SUN RISE
FROM THE BOTTOM OF THE SEA ...
BUT FIRST, ARE YOU EXPERIENCED?
HAVE YOU EVER BEEN EXPERIENCED?
WELL, I HAVE.

Imagination is the key to my lyrics, and the rest is painted with a little science fiction. What I like to do is write a lot of mythical scenes, like the history of the wars on Neptune and the reason Saturn's rings are there. You can write your own mythology.

Third Stone From The Sun is Earth. That's what it is. You have Mercury, Venus and then Earth. These guys come from another planet and they observe Earth for a while, and they think that the smartest animals on the whole Earth are chickens. There's nothing else here to offer. They don't really see anything that's worth taking. They don't like the people so much, so they just blow it up at the end.

One song called *I Don't Live Today* is dedicated to the American Indian and all minority repressed groups. That one is a "freak-out" tune. I might as well say that because everyone else is going to anyway. Do you want to know the meaning of that? I'll tell you, but don't think anything bad. "Freak-out" was old Californian lingo for humping in the back seat of a car. That's what it means, sexual perversion. Anyway, that's what it used to mean. I'm being very frank, that's all, so I guess I'll get deported soon.

Manic Depression is ugly times music. It's so ugly you can feel it. It's a story about a cat wishing he could make love to music instead of the same old everyday woman. A frustrating type of song for you, a today's type of blues.

The English music nature calls for pounds and pounds of melody. Irish folk songs call for complicated melodies. I'm from America. Blues is my backbone, and that doesn't call for as much melody. It calls for more rhythm, more down-to-earth hard feeling, whatever you call it – soul. Everybody wants to know what American soul is. Everybody thinks it's Motown. I think it's gotta end there. American soul is something like *Red House.* It's the kind of R&B number that might make the top 500. Yes, I like that one. We have more where that came from.

And then we have songs like *Foxy Lady*. I'm not ashamed to say I can't write happy songs. I don't feel very happy when I start writing. *Foxy Lady* is about the only happy song I've written. The microphone was set up and I had these words and we just started playing. We messed about with it a couple of times, and we were bouncing stuff around in our minds. If you get a good idea you have to put it down right away.

We have all these different sounds, but all of them are made from just nothing but a guitar, bass and drums, and slowed-down voices. The feedback you hear is from a straight amp and a little fuzz thing I had built. We don't even use an oscillator. That could really blow a lot of minds ...

It was mostly Chas Chandler and Eddie Kramer who worked on that stuff. Eddie was the engineer, and Chas as producer mainly kept things together. Maybe some of the stuff is far ahead, I don't know. I'm very happy with it, but already I can hardly wait for something else.

{ARE YOU EXPERIENCED? WAS IN THE U.K. CHARTS FOR THIRTY-THREE WEEKS, REACHING A TOP POSITION OF #2 BEHIND THE BEATLES' SGT. PEPPER'S LONELY HEARTS CLUB BAND. IN THE SECOND HALF OF MAY, THE EXPERIENCE BROKE ATTENDANCE RECORDS WHEN THEY PLAYED IN GERMANY, DENMARK AND SWEDEN.}

I like Sweden. The concerts have been much more successful than we could have expected for a first visit. When we played the Tivoli Gardens, the P.A. system was very bad, and the audience didn't really help us too much. But the second job we did later on that night was very, very good. The kids are great. They sit still and listen to my music, and I believe they understand it.

Sweden is the most beautiful country on earth. Some people would bore themselves to death there, especially younger people, because there isn't much to do. But that's the greatest thing it has to offer, peace and quiet. For resting, it's fantastic. And the girls are so much nicer than anywhere else. You can have nice and decent conversations with them, by which I don't mean to say you can't do that with girls from other countries, just that you can do that so much better with Swedish girls.

Sweden showed me more than anything so far. We heard some of these cats in little country clubs and little caves blowing some sounds that you can barely imagine. Every once in a while they start going like a wave. They get into each other within their personalities, and then the party last night or the hangover, the "evil," starts pulling them away again. You can hear it start to go away. Then it starts coming together again. It's like a wave, I guess, coming in and out.

{At the beginning of June 1967, the Experience played at the Palais de Sports pop festival in Paris and then returned to London for shows at the Saville Theatre, interviews and photo sessions.}

We want to be controversial. We are not "nice boys," and we do not play "sweet music." We don't believe in rehearsing. Rehearsals are only to see how the amps sound or something technical like that. We don't want to plan our music. It should be a surprise, for us as well as the audience. Besides, there are no rehearsal halls who will accept us anymore. They say we play too loud!

I know exactly what I'm doing when we're onstage. I don't try to move an audience. It's up to them what they get from the music. You can feel it as soon as you get out there. You can actually feel it before you hit the first note. Then, when you hit the first note, you can find out just where you're at.

If the people help us out, we can really get it together. But if they're going to sit up there and pantomime themselves, well, I just don't give a damn. After all, I'm not trying to give out a message to anybody.

If an audience is really digging you, then naturally you get excited, and it helps. But a bad audience doesn't really bother me. Then it's a practice session, a chance to get things together. If they have paid to see us, then we are going to do our thing. If we add a bit of the trampoline side of entertainment, then that is a fringe benefit. But we are there to play the music. I always enjoy playing, and I don't even care if they boo – as long as they boo in key!

At the moment, people don't have mixed feelings about us. They either like us or they don't. If someone criticizes my music – well, it depends who it is. If they don't understand it, this is because I am two years ahead of them, or it may be that I am two years behind! I don't give a damn so long as I have enough to eat and to play what I want to play. That's enough for me.

I consider ourselves to be some of the luckiest cats alive, because we're playing just what we want to play and people seem to like that. I haven't set out to produce a commercial sound. I don't even know what a hit record sounds like. I really want to continue playing and recording what gives me pleasure. I don't ever want to have to bow to commercialism.

YOU MUST REMEMBER that Jimi Hendrix U.S.A. didn't really have a chance to do anything because he was playing behind people. Then this happened – thanks to Chas and Mike Jeffery, really. They were the ones who had the faith that I could make it over here. When Chas saw me in Greenwich Village he said it would all happen, just like it has.

Britain is our station now. It's not my home, but it was our beginning, our birth. They took us in like lost babies. We'll stay here probably until around the end of June, then we'll see if we can get something going in America. We've been told that we'll do well, but I'm not sure we will be accepted as readily there. People are much more narrow-minded than they are in Britain. In the States the disc jockeys stopped playing *Hey Joe* because people complained about the lyrics. If they do like us, great! If not, too bad!

I arrived here with just the suit I stood up in. I'm going back with the best wardrobe of gear that Carnaby Street can offer. Noel and Mitch will go over great in the U.S. They'll love them so much they won't have to wash their own socks.

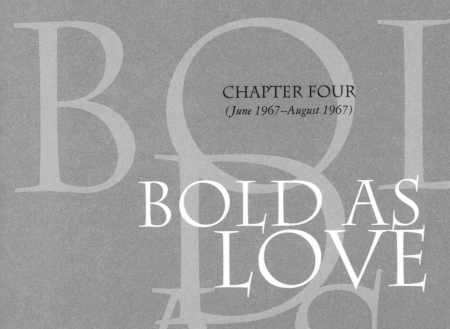

CHAPTER FOUR
(June 1967–August 1967)

BOLD AS LOVE

I'M NOT HERE TO DESTROY ANYTHING.
DON'T FORGET THERE ARE OTHER PEOPLE STILL
AROUND
MAKING THOSE NICE SWEET SOUNDS.
YOU'VE STILL GOT THE BEACH BOYS
AND THE FOUR SEASONS
TO HANG ON TO.

JUNE 18, 1967, MONTEREY, CALIFORNIA.

Paul McCartney was the big bad Beatle,

the beautiful cat who got us the gig at the Monterey Pop Festival.

That was our start in America.

ONTEREY WAS PREDOMINANTLY A MUSIC FESTIVAL, done up the way it's supposed to be done up.

Everything was perfect.

I said, "Wow! Everything's together!

What am I gonna do?"

In other words, I was scared at that almost. I was scared to go up there and play in front of all those people. You really want to turn those people on. It's just like a feeling of really deep concern. You get very intense. That's the way I look at it. That's natural for me. Once you hit the first note, or once the first thing goes down, then it's all right. Let's get to those people's butts!

Music makes me high onstage, and that's the truth. It's almost like being addicted to music. You see, onstage I forget everything, even the pain. Look at my thumb – how ugly it's become. While I'm playing I don't think about it. I just lay out there and jam. That's what it's all about, filling up the chest cavities and the empty kneecaps and the elbows.

It's another way of communication, of trying to make harmony amongst the people. When they feel and smile with that sleepy exhausted look, it's like being carried on a wave. You get into such a pitch sometimes that you go up into another thing. You don't forget about the audience, but you forget about all the paranoia, that thing where you're saying, "Oh gosh, I'm onstage – what am I going to do now?" Then you go into this other thing, and it turns out to be almost like a play in certain ways. I have to hold myself back sometimes because I get so excited – no, not excited, involved.

When I was in Britain I used to think about America every day. I'm American. I wanted people here to see me. I also wanted to see whether we could make it back here. And we made it, man, because we did our own thing, and it really was our own thing and nobody else's. We had our beautiful rock-blues-country-funky-freaky sound, and it was really turning people on. I felt like we were turning the whole world on to this new thing, the best, most lovely new thing. So I decided to destroy my guitar at the end of the song as a sacrifice. You sacrifice things you love.

I love my guitar.

THE MONTEREY FESTIVAL WAS A GOOD SCENE. All those beautiful people. We had a few days off, and then we did the Fillmore West. Then we played for nothing [Golden Gate Park in San Francisco], and I really enjoyed it too. Those flower people are really groovy. All the bands playing for free, that's what I call groovy teamwork. It was one of the best gigs we've ever played, and it sold ten thousand albums for us!

Flower Power! Yeah!

I wonder what we'll get next?
I suppose we'll get weed speed,
and then I can't wait for the winter when we'll get all those
fog songs and sledge-heads on the scene.

It's having fun though. I dig anything as long as it doesn't hurt anybody, but anything as long as people are grooving off it. You're not a love-in person just because you have curly hair or wear bells and beads. You have to believe in it, not just throw flowers. It's the feeling, and someone who wears a stiff white collar can have it.

Although the flower scene was all tied up with sensation stuff about drugs, the "love everybody" basic idea helped one hell of a lot with the color problem in the States. Colored artists didn't dare go near some southern audiences in the past. But since the flower power craze much of the violence has gone. Of course, a lot of those hippies may get busted once in a while, but you don't hear of banks being robbed by the hippies in California, do you?

I love the West Coast. That's where I'd like to live. The weather's nice, and there's lots of funny little people. I like the cars, man, beautiful cars. Not too many Volkswagens, which is good. Oh yeah, I nearly forgot – the girls. They even come down to the gigs. It's beautiful, it's ridiculous and all this other stuff, but I don't know what is happening at all!

WE HAD A GREAT TIME IN LOS ANGELES. We stayed at Peter Tork's house. It had about a thousand rooms, a couple of baths and two balconies that overlook the world and Piccadilly Circus. There's a stereo that makes you feel you are in a recording emporium, with an electric piano and guitars and amplifiers all over the place. There's a carport in which there is a Mercedes, a GTO and something that looks like an old copper stove. And a cute lovely little yellow puppy-type dog.

Dave Crosby and a group called the Electric Flag came round to see us at the Whisky A Go Go. Electric Flag are real groovy. One guy, Buddy Miles, is someone I like talking music with. I'm turned on to different things now, from the Electric Flag to Jefferson Airplane. I dig Jefferson Airplane's sound, but they shouldn't work for their lights. They've so much talent, yet sometimes their light shows are so good that the group becomes only 25 percent of what's happening. They become nothing but shadows, nothing but voices to the light patterns. I don't like that kind of thing blasting away throughout my act, but something different to illustrate each song would be nice – candles on stage for *The Wind Cries Mary*, a film for *Purple Haze* and so on.

{July 1967, first tour of America}

Then we got into a tour with the Monkees. They're like plastic Beatles. The Beatles are one group you really can't put down, because they're just too much, and it's so embarrassing when America is sending over the Monkees. They're a commercial product of American show business. Oh God! Dishwater! I really hate somebody like that to make it so big when they've got groups in the States that are starving to death trying to get breaks.

Don't get me wrong, I like the Monkees themselves. The personal part was beautiful. They're such good cats. I got on well with Micky and Peter, and we fooled around a lot together. All the rumors about being segregated on the plane were just nonsense.

We played seven performances with them, then pulled out of the tour because there was a hassle. Firstly, we were not getting any billing – all the posters for the show just screamed out MONKEES! They didn't even know we were there until we hit the stage. Then they gave us the "death" spot on the show – right before the Monkees were due on. The audience just screamed and yelled for the Monkees.

Finally they agreed to let us go on first, and things were much better. We got screams and good reactions, and some kids even rushed the stage. The kids started digging us more than the plastic Beatles!

Then some parents who brought their young kids complained that our act was vulgar.

They'd say, "What is this all about – kid's rushing that!?
Ugh! Too erotic!"

I am bemused by the whole thing. I suppose I might move around in certain ways, and girls in the front seats might have funny expressions on their faces, but it's not downright sexy. I believe it might have something to do with just the idea of somebody being on stage and showing themselves, and the people knowing they can't really touch them but they would like to. It's a frustrated feeling, but it's a good feeling. They probably don't get a chance to scream until this one time, and then they let EVERYTHING out.

We hadn't really played to that kind of kids' audience before, and you have to realize that though the parents of the kids in England don't interfere too much, the parents in the States are something else. And then there are all those different kinds of stuffy organizations over here, right? In New York the Daughters of the American Revolution tried to stop our show because they said we were too sexy. Imagine how these old ladies must have been turned on. They were turned on so bad they had to try and stop us from doing our thing. So this is where it's at now!

We decided it was just the wrong audience. I think they replaced me with **Mickey Mouse.**

MERICA'S JUST LIKE ANY OTHER COUNTRY. It just takes a little more time. We did different little places around like the club scene in New York, Central Park; Washington, D.C.; Ann Arbor, Michigan; and the Hollywood Bowl. We didn't know where we were sometimes.

We were taken around a little with the Mamas and Papas. In New York we all went out to the Electric Circus club in the Village, which completely blew my mind. There was a group called the Seeds playing there, but they had all these funny little acts going on between things. One guy walked up onto the stage and stood there and growled for about five minutes. Then he said, "Thank you" and walked off! There was another guy who came on in a straitjacket and just rolled around on the floor for half an hour.

Then some funny little guys came swinging down on ropes from the ceiling. We couldn't believe it! The Village Fugs are real crazy. They do things arranged from William Burroughs, songs about lesbians and things like freaking out with a barrel of tomatoes, squashing them all between your armpits. *Euuuggghh!* You'd never believe it, man, those cats are downright vulgar. They tell these nasty, beautiful poems, the nastiest ones you can think of.

Yeah, it was a really groovy time in the States. Except I got pulled up by the police in Washington, D.C. and I was refused entry to one or two restaurants, but that was because I was with a couple of hippies. One of them looked like Sitting Bull. It wasn't a racial thing.

*　　　*　　　*　　　*　　　*　　　*

In New York taxi drivers would drive up to me, take a look at my appearance then drive away. Some of these guys want everybody to be the same conforming type as themselves. Well, they ain't gonna catch me like that. *Why should I be like the taxi driver?*

I was completely unknown in America until the word got back that the British dug my kind of music. Now it's sellout business here. At the clubs in Greenwich Village we were welcomed like gods. Nobody who is continually experimenting with music makes big money, but they get respect in the right quarters.

I don't do anything all that different, but suddenly the magazines like **LIFE** and **TIME** are writing about me. It's a funny feeling. These are the same people who first laughed. Ha, Ha! Now I'm not stupid Jimi anymore, I'm Mr. Hendrix. They try to analyze me and come up with a psychiatrist's report, and it doesn't sound like me one little bit. They don't know what's running through my blood. We live in a different world. My world? That's hunger. It's the slums, raging race hatred, and the only happiness is the kind you can hold in your hand.

* * * *

CRITICS REALLY GIVE ME A PAIN IN THE NECK. It's like shooting at a flying saucer as it tries to land, without giving the occupants a chance to identify themselves! There'll always be somebody who wants to nail you down. They come back to the dressing room with a kind of `"let's strip him naked and hang him from a tall tree"` attitude. Most of them go away so stoned they don't know what they're writing about.

They are already classifying us on the basis of one album and perhaps one or two concerts they've heard. It's not easy to classify us, but sure as hell they are going to try! Like, somebody called me the "Black Elvis." It's the establishment's game. Pat us on the back and get rid of us quick. Squeeze the soul out of us and put us in cages for the rest of our lives. But we won't be put in! We don't pay attention to brand names like that. Once they have you thinking about yourself, they have you by the balls.

Something different like the Experience comes along, and a lot of labelers are frightened by it. They want to put you in little bags. If they can't put you in a bag, then they're frightened and don't know what to do. Quite naturally they're going to start little rumors about people they don't understand, like *"Jimi Hendrix is sullen, he's always stoned, he drinks watermelon juice with his coffee, he uses shower curtains for toilet paper."* This is what the negative folks are trying to tell you. They project a certain image so everybody gets scared to actually know about me.

It's going to take time to reach these labelers with our sounds. For starters I don't think you should try to dissect the musical and the visual.

People who put down our performance are people who can't use their eyes and ears at the same time. They've got a button on their shoulder blades that keeps only one working at a time. You feel they're kind of afflicted, like a cat who can't watch TV and chew gum. **Damn them and those crummy bird-crumb snatchers who say I don't really play with my teeth!**

WHEN WE GOT TOGETHER IN ENGLAND we didn't say, "All right, now we're going to play this song, I think I'll go down on my knees, and Mitch, you twirl your sticks there, and Noel, you put the bass on top of your head." We just got thrown together. We didn't know each other from Adam, and all these things started happening.

What it is, is self-satisfaction. We're playing for the audience, but I have to entertain myself too. And I'm working for that note to come out a little different. Sometimes I have to wind it up physically to feel that note. If I feel like putting the guitar down and stepping on it, I'll do it. Same with Noel. He plays his guitar any kind of way he feels.

If I stopped moving around because some people were distracted from the music, I would be dishonest and give myself ten points less. We might play sometimes just standing there. Sometimes we do the whole diabolical bit when we're in the studio and there's nobody to watch. It's how we feel. How we feel, and getting the music out. The sooner people understand that the better.

And I think it's time for people to understand that we are not always in the same bag with each performance. How can you be when you are constantly reaching, improvising, experimenting? It's impossible. In the old days we used to go on with a list, but pretty soon I threw the list away because I didn't feel like it. Spontaneity is what I could best term it. We are constantly growing in this spontaneity. This whole thing's going to blow wide open soon.

Things have to go through me, and I have to show my feelings as soon as they're there. That's why when we played at Monterey I decided to burn my guitar. I'd just finished painting the guitar that day and was really into it. I sprayed lighter fluid on it and then stamped out the burning pieces. It went over pretty well, so in Washington, D.C., I destroyed my guitar again. When we played the Hollywood Bowl they were waiting for us with fire extinguishers!

THE SMASHING ROUTINE BEGAN BY ACCIDENT. I was playing in Copenhagen, and I got pulled off stage. Everything was going great. I threw my guitar back onto the stage and jumped back after it. When I picked it up there was a great crack down the middle. I just lost my temper and smashed the damn thing to pieces.

The crowd went mad – you'd have thought I'd found the "lost chord" or something. After that, whenever the press was about or I got that feeling, I just did the bit again. But it isn't just for the show, and I can't explain the feeling. It's just like you want to let loose and do exactly what you want if your parents weren't watching.

I'm not really a violent man, but people got the impression I was because of the act. You do this destruction thing maybe three or four times, and everybody thinks you do it all the time. We only do it when we feel like it. You feel very frustrated, and the music gets louder and louder, and all of a sudden, crash, bang, it goes up in smoke. Some nights we can be really bad. If we smash something up then, it's because that instrument, which is something you dearly love, just isn't working that night. It's not responding, so you want to kill it. It's a love-hate relationship, just like you feel at times when your girlfriend starts messing around. You can do it because the music and the instrument can't fight back.

It's just the bad bits coming out in me. I mean, no matter how sweet and lovely you are, there are black and ugly things deep down somewhere. I bring mine out on stage, and that way no one gets hurt. And we find that it works for the audience too. We try to drain all the violence out of their systems. We mostly build on bar patterns and emotion, not melody. We can play violent music, and in a way it releases their violence. It's not like beating it out of each other, but like violent silk. I mean, sadness can be violent.

Maybe after people dig us presenting some violence on stage they won't want to leave and destroy the outside world. Feeling vibrations and letting loose at a place like that is a soul-bending type of thing. It's better than bending your soul in riots. **You should never get to that point.**

{THE SUMMER OF 1967 WAS MARRED BY THE WORST RACIAL VIOLENCE OF THE DECADE. THE EXPERIENCE PLAYED IN DETROIT ON AUGUST 15, SHORTLY AFTER RACE RIOTS HAD DEVASTATED MUCH OF THE CITY AND LEFT FORTY-TWO DEAD.}

THE NEGRO RIOTS IN THE STATES ARE CRAZY. Discrimination is crazy. I think we can live together without these problems, but because of the violence these problems aren't solved yet. There's a lot of silly talk on both sides. Quite naturally I don't like to see houses being burned, but I don't have too much feeling for either side right now.

There is no such thing as a color problem. It is a weapon for the negative forces who are trying to destroy the country. They make black and white fight against each other so they can take over at each end. That is what the establishment is waiting for. They let you fight, they let you go out into the streets and riot. But they'll still put you in jail. I wish they'd had electric guitars in the cotton fields back in the good old days. A whole lot of things would have been straightened out, not just for the black and white, but I mean for the cause.

LOOK AT THE SKY TURN A HELL-FIRE RED, LORD
SOMEBODY'S HOUSE IS BURNING
DOWN, DOWN, DOWN, DOWN.

WELL, I ASKED MY FRIEND,
"WHERE IS THAT BLACK SMOKE COMING FROM?"
HE JUST COUGHED AND CHANGED THE SUBJECT AND SAID,
"UH, IT MIGHT SNOW SOME."

SO I LEFT HIM SIPPING HIS TEA
AND I JUMPED IN MY CHARIOT AND RODE OFF
TO SEE JUST WHY AND WHO COULD IT BE THIS TIME.
SISTERS AND BROTHERS, DADDIES,
MOTHERS STANDIN' ROUND CRYING.
WHEN I REACHED THE SCENE THE FLAMES
WERE MAKING A GHOSTLY WHINE.
SO I STOOD ON MY HORSE'S BACK
AND I SCREAMED WITHOUT A CRACK,
I SAY, "OH BABY, WHY'D YOU BURN
YOUR BROTHER'S HOUSE DOWN?"

WELL, SOMEONE STEPPED FROM THE CROWD,
HE WAS NINETEEN MILES HIGH.
HE SHOUTS, "WE'RE TIRED AND DISGUSTED,
SO WE PAINT RED THROUGH THE SKY."
I SAY, "THE TRUTH IS STRAIGHT AHEAD,
SO DON'T BURN YOURSELF INSTEAD,
TRY TO LEARN INSTEAD OF BURN, HEAR WHAT I SAY!"

You know where the truth is. The truth is that it's time to get together now! If people would only stop blaming. You can see how frustrating it is. The black person argues with the white person that he's been treated badly for the last two hundred years. Well, he has, but now's the time to work it out instead of talking about the past. We know that the past is all screwed up, so instead of talking about it, let's get things together now!

AUGUST 8, 1967, *BURNING OF THE MIDNIGHT LAMP* RELEASED IN THE U.S.}

I really don't care what our records do as far as chart-wise. *Burning Of The Midnight Lamp*, which everyone around here hated, only made number eleven in the charts. They said that was the worst record, but to me that was the best one we ever made. I think it's a very groovy record. I'm glad it didn't get big and get thrown around. A lot of nice records get abused through the charts. They throw them up to the top three, and then they come right back down. It might have been a nice record, but nobody will remember it two weeks from now.

I don't think that people really understood *Burning Of The Midnight Lamp*. Maybe it's a little murky in there, a bit smoky, but it's the kind of disc you put down and go back to. When I first heard Procol Harum's *Whiter Shade Of Pale*, the meaning was very muddy. I understood about the first verse and that was all. But as you hear it again and again, you begin to put the thing together.

I wrote part of that song on a plane between L.A. and New York and finished it in the studios in New York. There are some very personal things in there. I was feeling kind of down. But I think that everyone can understand the feeling that when you're traveling, no

102

matter what your address, there is no place you can call home. The feeling of a man in a little old house in the middle of a desert where he is burning the midnight lamp. You don't mean for things to be personal all the time, but that's the way it is ...

THE MORNING IS DEAD AND THE DAY IS TOO.
THERE'S NOTHING LEFT HERE TO GREET ME BUT THE VELVET MOON.
ALL MY LONELINESS I HAVE FELT TODAY.
IT'S A LITTLE MORE THAN ENOUGH TO MAKE
A MAN THROW HIMSELF AWAY.
AND I CONTINUE TO BURN THE MIDNIGHT LAMP, ALONE.

NOW THE SMILING PORTRAIT OF YOU
IS STILL HANGING ON MY FROWNING WALL
BUT IT REALLY DOESN'T, REALLY DOESN'T BOTHER ME, TOO MUCH AT ALL.
IT'S JUST THE EVER FALLING DUST THAT MAKES IT SO HARD FOR ME TO SEE
THAT FORGOTTEN EARRING LAYING ON THE FLOOR
FACING COLDLY TOWARDS THE DOOR
AND I CONTINUE TO BURN THE MIDNIGHT LAMP ALL ALONE.

I can't stay in one place too long. It drags me down, regardless of what's happening. I'm scared of vegetating. I have to move on. There's so much to see and so many places to go. I wish I could travel all the time. I was in England longer than I've stayed in any one place, other than New York. I dig Britain, but I haven't really got a home anywhere. **The Earth's my home.**

EZY RIDER

THERE GOES EZY, EZY RIDER
RIDING DOWN THE HIGHWAY
OF DESIRE
HE SAYS THE FREE WIND
TAKES HIM HIGHER
TRYING TO FIND HIS HEAVEN ABOVE
BUT HE'S DYING
TO BE LOVED.

{JIMI FLEW TO LONDON ON AUGUST 10, 1967, AND THE EXPERIENCE RETURNED
TO EUROPE FOR TV APPEARANCES AND CONCERTS.}

Everywhere I go I always try to meet people. People to talk with, to laugh with and to make music with. The one thing that's very important is people to talk with. But since I first came to Europe I've met one in a hundred people who let me talk about what I want to. Everybody asks me how old I am, if it's true I have Indian blood, how many women I've had, if I'm married, if I have a Rolls-Royce, or more of those jokes. The people who dig me don't want this at all. They want something different. They want to feel something inside, something real – revolution, struggle, rebellion. They know where you're at without asking questions. They know from the music. But there's no point in talking like this. I just stand about and wait for the next question, and people usually misconstrue my answers. I know what I mean, but I can't form the words.

IT SEEMS LIKE THE PEOPLE IN SCANDINAVIA just aren't ready for the way we look. In Sweden they moved us out of the hotel lobby just because Princess Alexandra was coming through! I guess the guy at the hotel thought we were a bit scruffy and tried to tidy the place up for the Princess. He was real cool. He invited us to have a drink. We play about ten places here, I guess. I'm not sure because I don't keep up with that. I just play. We're going to take a vacation soon, right after this Scandinavian tour.

We're working very, very hard now. Once you've made a name for yourself, you are all the more determined to keep it up. In any case, I don't believe you've really made it until you breathe your last breath.

So what we are trying to do is to be more and more progressive, to make our music and our act more varied and exciting, so that all age groups can enjoy it.

{IN NOVEMBER AND DECEMBER 1967, THE EXPERIENCE HEADED A PACKAGE TOUR OF BRITAIN, SUPPORTED BY THE MOVE, PINK FLOYD, AMEN CORNER, OUTER LIMITS, THE NICE AND EIRE APPARENT.}

Although I wasn't scared starting my first big tour, we did wonder how they would accept us, there being so many different acts and us probably the most extreme of all. In the clubs they would just come to see us, but on this tour you get all kinds and all ages. Like always, we go out to play and please the public, and so far it's been wild, really wild. In Blackpool the police slipped Mitch and Noel in through side doors and took me 'round the block five times before helping me in. I lost some hair, but I might have lost the lot if they hadn't been guarding me!

It's the best tour I've been on. Sometimes, while you're into your music, you might hear little teeny-weenies – little piglets – squealing out there. Sometimes they scream in the wrong places, like when I cough. I feel funny then. It's like, "Uh-oh, here they go." It's a little hard to explain what really bugs me about that scene. I mean, you don't perform according to how they scream.

The Nice are my favorite group on this tour. Their sound is ridiculously good – original, free, more funky than West Coast. You don't have the West Coast scene in Britain, at least not out in the open. The Underground is where it's in the groove. And over here if it's not Engelbert Humperdink, it's Underground.

THE BLINDFOLD TEST:

"Strange Brew" (Cream). *Oh, I know who that is all right, by the first note! Ooh, that's nice. Was that a horn in the background? Those voices and the guitar sound so well together. It has a strange kind of West Coast and San Francisco sound. Eric's guitar is sounding funkier and more relaxed. He's gradually changing, but with a cat like that you can never tell when he's going to settle down. It could be disastrous if he did. This is a nice blues song that you can dig between Engelbert and Cat Stevens on the radio. I like this record, but I don't know about the little kiddies. The Cream shouldn't worry though, because they are playing what they like. Groups like Cream, Traffic and Family are so deeply interested in their music that they are creating a culture. Their music is so important to them.*

"Loving You" (Billy Fury). *Is that an English guy singing? It's not Billy J. Kramer? Not whatshisname – Billy Fury? He sings very nicely, and it's the sound I used to like when I was a little boy. It could have been a stronger arrangement to help him out. That's an old Elvis Presley song. At least Billy is getting his name back. It's nice.*

"Come To The Sunshine" (Harpers Bizarre). *That's an English group too? Weird little voices. Who could it be? Oh, what was that sound? I don't know, that's almost like a fairy tale, a theme for a children's movie. You can take it off now if you want to. That's not for me, but there's no telling. It might sell twenty million. It's one of those goody-goody records with a completely commercial sound, no feeling, no nothing. It's just made to sell records.*

"What Good Am I?" (Cilla Black). *It sounds like a female Tim Hardin. Now it's changed complexion. God, it must be Cilla Black. Now it makes me think of Sonny and Cher. Yes, I like that. Her voice sounds like controlled feedback, it's so powerful. Now she sounds like Dionne Warwick! God, what's happening nowadays? Yes, there's a nice feeling on this.*

"Here Come The Nice" (Small Faces). *I've heard these voices somewhere before. The lead singer sounds very nice. That has to be the Small Faces. I was going to ask if they had a girl in the group! Their music is very funky, but it sounded like a girl's voice at the beginning. This has a very good beat. The backing voices and the drumming give it away. God, what's happening there? They are doing one of those Mrs. Miller tricks, slowing down the speed. That's slowed-down soprano! It's pretty hard to say if that will be a hit. I've met the little cats in the group. They're all so little. When I first came here they were really happening, but now they don't seem to be doing too much. I hope they come through all right because they are a very good group, especially image-wise. They should feature their lead singer more. I'd like to try and write some songs for them.*

"She's Leaving Home" (Beatles). *Who's that? It's not the Beatles, it's too commercial. The voices are a little more steady, and they've got echo on the violins. It's an English group trying to sound like the Beatles. Sounds like Ringo to me. Ringo hasn't gone solo, has he? This is one of the most commercial songs on the album. The Beatles LP is standard equipment for all the groups at the moment. Everybody is so worried about the Beatles and where they are going. It's so silly. Just take the music for what it's worth. I wish we could end up like them!*

I T SEEMS TO ME LIKE MUSIC GOES IN A BIG CYCLE, and it's coming back to more of a true form of music now. During a certain age, which was past not so long ago, they started getting really superficial and junky. This was because the music started getting too complicated. In order to get into that you have to be really true to yourself, and none of those cats were doing that. The idea is not to get as complicated as you can but to get as much of yourself into it as you can. I feel everything I play. It's a release of all my inner feelings – aggression, tenderness, sympathy, everything. Same with Noel and Mitch. It's a wedding of our feelings in music. We all three have our own little scene as far as music goes. One of us is in a rock bag, another is just jazz, while I'm in the blues. We are all doing our separate things together. This way everything's a very natural progression.

Music has to go places. That's why we make something new. It's hard for me to think in terms of blues anymore. The content of the old blues was singing about sex and booze. Now people are saying so much more with music. Motown isn't the real sound of any Negro artist singing. It's so commercial, so put together, so beautiful, that I don't feel anything from it. All they do, and this is my own opinion, is put a very hard beat to it, a very good beat. Then they put about a thousand people on tambourines, plus a thousand horns and a thousand violins, and then a singer overdubs his voice millions of times, and to me it comes out so artificial. "Synthetic Soul" is what I call Motown.

I really don't like the word "soul" in connection with the Experience. A Spanish dancer has soul. Everybody has soul. Music is nobody's soul. It's something from somebody's real heart. It doesn't necessarily mean physical notes that you hear by ear. It could be notes that you hear by feeling or by thought or by imagination or even by emotions. I like the words "feeling" and "vibration." I get very hung up on this feeling bag. **The sounds of a funky guitar just thrill me, go all through me. I can get inside it almost. I'm not saying that I play that good; I'm just explaining my feeling towards it and the feelings towards the sound it produces.**

I've got about eight guitars,
but the two I use are the Fender
Stratocaster and a Gibson Flying
Angel, which is shaped like a letter
A and is extremely rare in Britain. I
play a Fender Stratocaster because
it gets used pretty hard in the act and it's the only one which
will stand up to it. Everybody's screaming about the
seven-year-old Telecaster and the twelve-year-old
Gibson and the ninety-two-year-old Les Paul.
They've gone into an age bag now, but it's nothing
but a fad. The guitars nowadays play just as good.
You know, the salesman is always telling you that
Chuck Berry took this one to the bathroom with him
and he didn't have any toilet paper, so watch out for
the pick guard. § **I tried the Telecaster**, and it only has
two sounds, good and bad, and a very weak tone variation.
The Guild guitar is very delicate, but it has one of the best
sounds. I tried one of the new Gibsons, but I literally couldn't play
it at all, so I'll stick with my Fender. § **The Stratocaster** is the best
all-round guitar for the stuff we're doing. You can get the very bright
trebles and the deep bass sound. I use light-gauge strings, and I put them
on slightly higher so they can ring longer. I don't like to use mikes. To
get the right sound it's a combination of both amp and fretting. It's a
simple trick. I turn the amplifier knob really fast once, twice. That gives
the singing, whistling tone – the electronic tone. The trick then is to
control this tone with the fingers. It doesn't make any difference
what size the amps are as long as I know I have it. **I'm not
necessarily trying to be loud. I'm just
trying to get this impact.**

111

"I'd like to warn you now,
it's going to be a bit loud,
a teeny bit loud,
because these are English amps and we're in Sweden,
and the electricity scene is not working out
with this Australian fuzz tone
and this American guitar ..."

As long as the equipment holds up, we're fine. We have so much trouble with amplifiers. We have to get them overhauled after every trip. We're always playing out of the shadows and ashes of the last gig we did. We've just come off a tour, and I think we went through about four Marshalls. This is about the fifth set, and they've really had it. They've been screwed properly. I've got about four speakers left and about three more valve tubes. And Mitch Haze is on his third pair of arms!

It really brings me down when the amps don't work, and it makes me twice as mad when a road manager tries to tell me, just because they're fucked up, that they're overworking too much. I'm not an amp repair man, but if they begin to buzz or give us any trouble, we do an instant repair job – we kick them in!

I really like my old Marshall tube amps because when it's working properly there's nothing can beat it, nothing in the whole world. It looks like two refrigerators hooked together. When I was in Greenwich Village I had a Fender amp and an old extension loudspeaker, and it made the weirdest sounds. That's when I first started using feedback. I fooled with it, and what I'm doing now is the fruit of my fooling around. It's mostly feedback and the way you control the knobs.

See, you can take a plate off the back here and tap these little springs, and it makes these weird little sounds. Then we use repeat echo and wah-wah, you know, things like that. The wah-wah pedal is great because it doesn't have any notes. Nothing but hitting it straight up, using the vibrato. Then the drums come through, and it feels like, not depression, but that loneliness and that frustration, that yearning for something, like something is reaching out.

The first record I heard with wah-wah was *Tales Of Brave Ulysses.* Two or three days after Cream came out with that one we released our first LP, and on the track *I Don't Live Today* there's a guitar solo that's wah-wah like. But we were using a hand wah-wah then. It was coincidental because we didn't know anything about their record and they didn't know anything about ours.

The way I play lead is a raw type of way, and it just comes to you naturally. But the most essential thing to learn is the time, the rhythm. They got millions of beautiful solo guitarists in the world now, playing really beautiful greasy solos, but some of them are forgetting their rhythm section, and it's getting really monotonous to hear. Eric Clapton is a great guitarist and we think along the same lines, but I'm not sure he's playing exactly what he wants to. I was jamming with Eric the other day and it was pretty nice, but I wanted to hear him bring out some chords!

I only heard one record by Jeff Beck, *Shapes Of Things.* I really dug it, but I wasn't really influenced by it. I listen to everybody, but I don't try to copy anybody. Cats I like now are Albert King and Elmore James, but if you try to copy them note for note your mind starts wandering. Therefore, you dig them, and then do your own thing. Other musicians are doing so much in their own way. There's one cat I'm still trying to get across to people. His name is Albert Collins. He's buried in a road band somewhere. He's good, really good, but he's a family cat and doesn't want to go too far from home. Ain't that always the way?

I've never tried to establish one sound as a guitarist. You always knew it was Chuck Berry or Duane Eddy or Bo Diddley when they played. But I'm trying to get new things all the time. Whatever you do, you have to have an open mind. Anybody who's hungry, who's young and wants to get into music, has got so much to be influenced by, so many different things in the world. But some cats want to be helped every inch of the way. If you want to get there the work must come from you, even though another guy can maybe give you a bit of help or some good advice. You can get started on somebody else's back, but you end up having to go your own way.

I like the guitar best. It's part of me now. But it's not necessarily guitar that I'm interested in. It's my music I'm trying to get across. Music is very serious to me. It's my way of saying what I want to say. I hear sounds, and if I don't get them together, nobody else will.

{VOTED "WORLD'S TOP MUSICIAN" IN *MELODY MAKER* POLL.}

Me, the world's greatest!? That's silly.

Now, I appreciate them saying that, but it's pretty hard to say who the greatest is. I still can't figure it all out yet, because I've only been playing in Britain a year. I consider myself lucky I had a chance to be heard. There are so many good groups who haven't had a chance to be heard.

I don't care about what the critics say. I really don't give a damn about my future or career, I just want to make sure I can get out what I want. Soon I'll be going into another bag with a new sound, a new record, a new experience. We'll go exactly the way we feel. Nothing will be intentional. It'll just happen. We're not going to try and keep up with the trends, because we've got a chance to be our own trend.

I feel really respected to do something like this, but I'm still a bit worried. I think everyone should open their minds a bit to the fact that there are three of us in the group. There are two other cats working just as hard as I am. If it weren't for Mitch and Noel, I couldn't do my thing. Mitch particularly has so much to contribute. Primarily we are a group, and our new album, *Axis: Bold As Love,* is designed to show what else we do besides my guitar playing.

THE ALBUM WAS MADE over a period of sixteen days, which I'm very sad about. But we had to get it out to put in all the kiddies' stockings for Christmas. We were really deep into it, and all the songs on it are exactly the way we felt right then, so it really is us. We all helped in producing it with Chas Chandler, and I mixed it with him as well. It was mixed beautifully, but then we lost the original so we had to re-mix it the next morning within eleven hours, and it's very hard to do that. It could have been so much better. The songs could have been better too. As soon as you finish you get a hundred completely new ideas.

The only people that's on it is us three, except on one song, *You Got Me Floatin'*, one of the Move sang the background with Noel and Mitch. And that's our manager's big feet on the fade-out of *If Six Was Nine*. That was a complete jam session, and then we put the words on afterwards. Gary Leeds and Graham Nash did some foot stomping, and that's me on the flute. That's what you call a great feeling of blues, how you feel at a particular time.

I adore *If Six Was Nine*. It means that it really doesn't matter if everything is upside down as long as it doesn't bother you and you can cope with it. It doesn't say nothing bad about nobody. It just says let them go on and screw up theirs, just as long as they don't mess with me.

On *Spanish Castle Magic* Noel uses an eight-string bass. I was playing the same thing on the guitar in unison with the bass. It didn't come out as clear as we wanted it to, but it was a hint of what we were trying to do. It's a place you wouldn't put your grandmother, and it's dedicated to the plainclothes police and other goofballs.

On *Up From The Skies* it's thanks to Mitch for the jazz. It's the story of a guy who's been on earth before but on a different turning of the axis. Now he's come back to find this scene happening, like people laying up in gray buildings and so forth, dusting away. And people run around shouting, "Oh love the world, love the world!" eating rodent seeds and so forth. People must respect other people's ideas, as long as they're not hurting anybody. They must respect the time sequence. Why keep living in the past?

Personally, I like to write songs like *Castles Made Of Sand*. A lot of times you might get an idea from something you have seen, and then you write it down the way you might have wanted it to happen or the way it could have happened. It's like these buildings ain't going to be here for all that long. When it's time for a change, by all means put that thing into operation. I dig writing slow songs because I find it's easier to get more blues and feeling into them.

Little Wing is based on a very, very simple American Indian style. I got the idea when I was in Monterey, and I just happened to be looking at everything around. So I figured that I'd take everything I'd seen and put it, maybe, in the form of a girl and call it *Little Wing*. It'll just fly away. Everybody was flyin' and in a nice mood, like the police and everybody were really groovy out there. So I just took all these things and just put them in one very, very small little matchbox. Keep it just like that. It's very simple. I like it though. It's one of the very few I like.

In *Little Wing* we put the guitar through the Leslie speaker of an organ, and it sounds like jellybread. And we've got a gadget called the Octavia that we use on a song called *One Rainy Wish*. It comes through a whole octave higher so that when playing high notes it sometimes sounds like a whistle or a flute.

We've tried to get most of the freaky tracks right into another dimension, so you get that sky effect like they're coming down out of the heavens. Like on *Bold As Love*, we do something called phasing. It makes it sound like planes going through your membranes and chromosomes. A cat got that together accidentally, and he turned us onto it. It was a special sound, and we didn't want to use tapes of airplanes. We wanted to have the music itself warped.

But the secret of my sound is largely the electronic genius of our tame boffin, who is known to us as Roger the Valve [Roger Mayer]. He is an electronics man working in a government department, and he would probably lose his job if it was known he was working with a pop group. Whatever incredible sounds we think up, he manages to create them.

He has rewired my guitars in a special way to produce an individual sound, and he has made me a fantastic fuzz tone. I love different sounds as long as they're related to what we're trying to say or if they touch me in any way. I don't like to be gimmicky or different just for the sake of being different. Don't forget about the music. We don't.

Some people have told me that the first album sounded the same all the way through, but there wasn't time. It was a first one, a quick one, you understand, for a new group. In *Axis* there are more gentle things, more things for people to think about if they want to. It's quieter as far as guitar is concerned, but then we're emphasizing the words. I think we're getting less rebellious, if you know what I mean. To people who are not listening very much, *Axis* will put them to sleep right away.

I JUST THOUGHT ABOUT THE TITLE. There might be a meaning behind the whole thing. The axis of the earth turns around and changes the face of the world, and completely different civilizations come about or another age comes about. In other words, it changes the face of the earth, and it only takes about a quarter of a day.

Well, it's the same with love. It can turn your whole world upside down, like the axis of the earth. It's that powerful, that bold. People kill themselves for love. But when you have it for somebody or something, an idea maybe, it can beat anger and time and move the sea and the mountains. That's the way it feels. I guess that's what I'm trying to say.

ANGER, HE SMILES,
TOWERING IN SHINY METALLIC PURPLE ARMOR.
QUEEN JEALOUSY, ENVY, WAITS BEHIND HIM,
HER FIERY GREEN GOWN SNEERS AT THE GRASSY GROUND.
BLUE ARE THE LIFE-GIVING WATERS TAKING FOR GRANTED,
THEY QUIETLY UNDERSTAND.
ONCE HAPPY TURQUOISE ARMIES LAY OPPOSITE,
READY, BUT WONDERING WHY THE FIGHT IS ON.
BUT THEY'RE ALL BOLD AS LOVE,
THEY'RE BOLD AS LOVE.
JUST ASK THE AXIS.

MY RED IS SO CONFIDENT
HE FLASHES TROPHIES OF WAR AND RIBBONS OF EUPHORIA.
ORANGE IS YOUNG, FULL OF DARING,
BUT VERY UNSTEADY FOR THE FIRST GO-ROUND.
MY YELLOW IN THIS CASE IS NOT SO MELLOW.
IN FACT, I'M TRYING TO SAY THAT IT'S FRIGHTENED,
LIKE ME.
AND ALL THESE EMOTIONS OF MINE KEEP HOLDING ME
FROM GIVING MY LIFE TO A RAINBOW LIKE YOU.
BUT I'M BOLD AS LOVE,
WELL, I'M BOLD AS LOVE...
JUST ASK THE AXIS.
HE KNOWS EVERYTHING.

Sometimes you see things in different ways than other people, so then you write it in a song. It could represent anything. Like some feelings make you think of different colors. Jealousy is purple. I'm purple with rage or purple with anger. And green is envy. This is like explaining your different emotions in color towards this certain girl who has all the colors in the world. In other words, you don't think you have to part with these emotions but you're willing to try.

I get a lot of my inspiration for songs from girls. These girls are like one girl to me. Like *The Wind Cries Mary* is representing more than one person. And she's the one that really comes around. *Little Wing* was a very sweet girl that came around that gave me her whole life and more if I wanted it. And me with my crazy ass couldn't get it together, so I'm off here and off over there.

You can't hold on to relationships when living a raving life like me. I'm an adventurer traveling around the world looking for excitement. It's the same thing as the olden days when the war happens and you ride into town for the drinks and parties and so forth. You play your gig, and these beautiful girls come around and really entertain you. You do actually fall in love with them because that's the only love you can have.

When I was on the block starving it was the girls that used to help me. One of them even bought a guitar for me. Ever since then I say to myself, "Well, any girl I meet now I'm going to try to show her my appreciation!" Seriously though, it's just nature. You shouldn't be envious, because if you're not used to it, it could kill you really!

Sometimes it's a problem to be nice to all of them. If they invite you to their place and you say "no thanks," then they think you are big-timing them. And half of them ask you such silly questions, like when was the last time you saw John Lennon and can you get the Box Tops' autographs. There's also a big challenge thing with some girls. They'll say to their friends, boasting, "Oh, I've been with him before," and they'll say, "I wonder what it's like to sleep with John Walker?"

Some people call them "groupies." We call them "band aids." They are just innocent little girls trying to do their thing. But the establishment is so uptight about sex that all it wants to do is make the groupies look bad. So the insecure man puts labels on them — suck your favorite star. They don't talk about the ones who bring flowers and then go home to their mothers.

I'M THE BIGGEST SQUARE OF ALL when it comes to approaching someone I really dig. You don't go by appearance 'cause, boy, we know the story. Some of them are the worst people in the world. There are other things that girls have to offer besides their looks. The first thing I look for when meeting a girl is to see if she's human. It's so nice meeting girls not wearing masks, who dare to be kind.

I get sad about all the girls I see walking on the street when I'm in a taxicab, because I'll never meet them, and perhaps one of them is the right girl for me. I can fall in love, really in love, with one girl, and I can also fall in love with someone else, but in a different way at the same time. I guess I confuse myself sometimes.

MAY THIS BE LOVE OR JUST CONFUSION,
BORN OUT OF FRUSTRATION, WRACKED
FEELINGS OF NOT BEING ABLE TO
MAKE TRUE PHYSICAL LOVE TO
THE UNIVERSAL GYPSY QUEEN,
TRUE, FREE EXPRESSED MUSIC.
DARLING GUITAR
PLEASE REST.
A M E N

The guitar and music come first for me. Only then do I think about women. With music there's not time for anything else. I've no intention of getting married. I really couldn't imagine it. Marriage and other artificial forms that have been passed down generation to generation say it's bad to make love to a girl or whore or cross to the other side when you've been going berserk for years. Those are nothing but artificial rules. Those bits of paper called marriage certificates are only for people who feel insecure. You can give yourself to somebody, and you can take yourself away from somebody if you want to. But in a split second because, don't forget, it's your life.

Freedom is the key word to this whole thing. People don't understand that because their brains are too complex. Why do you think that every single human being on this earth is so different from every other one? There's a purpose behind this. Everybody has their own ways. They can do exactly what they want. When it's time for you to die, you've got to do it all by yourself. Nobody's going to help you.

Sweet words don't help nobody.

LETTER TO A FAN:

> *Regardless of what people think about you, just so long as you have your freedom of mind and freedom of speech and thought, don't let nobody turn you on your own thoughts and dreams. I am very interested in meeting you. I believe I would really love to talk to you for a very long time. You seem very different from other girls who may write to us. I believe your mind is really and truly together. BUT!! – don't call yourself stupid anymore in LIFE. This is your life. You must die by yourself, so for heaven's sake live for yourself and no one else.*

Love you forever,

Jimi Hendrix

Are you glad to be back in London?

> There's no place like London. Basically, I'm a country cat.
> I go crazy in the city, but then I don't consider London a city.
> It's more relaxing.

Why do you carry two dimes in your shoe?

> That was all I had when I landed in this country.

What do you think of the British police?

> I think the police are very groovy over here. They don't
> bother you very much. As a matter of fact I was walking down
> the street in London completely out of my mind, completely
> and utterly, and a police wagon came and they said, "Hi,
> Jimi, how are you doing?" and I replied, "Is it tomorrow –
> or just the end of time?"

Do you take LSD?

> Do I look like I do?

Why not?

> Because it's naked. I need oxygen.

How does the British hippie scene compare to that
in the States?

> The movement is not as organized over here. They've just
> got weird-looking cats. It's a small thing, not like it is in
> the States.

Do the teachings of Maharishi Mahesh Yogi appeal to you?
> I don't really believe that his transcendental meditation
> is much more than day dreaming. If you really believe
> in yourself, you can think it out on your own. You don't
> need someone else.

What do you do in your spare time?
> If I'm not working, I rarely leave the flat. Mostly I sit at
> home here playing records. I don't like having to dress up
> and go to social parties much, but you just have to do it.
> I always have the feeling that I will arrive at one of these
> things in all my own gear, and they might not let me in.
> I like to leave all that to the glamour people as far as possible,
> the Engelberts and Tom Joneses. They are the ones who sing
> beautifully enough to have their voices in TV commercials.
> Me, I'm just trying to get my music together.

What are your ambitions now?
> Oh, that changes a hundred times a day. You never know
> what shape clouds are going to be before you see them. I have
> only one life to live. I might not be here tomorrow, so I'm
> doing what I'm doing now. Because human beings die too
> easily, you know.

Do you like kids?
> Yeah, I like kids. I guess I like them any age.

What about old people?

> Some old people are a gas. In fact, a lot of older people are far groovier than some of my own generation. You're only as old as you think you are. As long as your mind can still function you're still young.

Can you think of yourself being eighty?

> I don't think I'll be around when I'm eighty. There's other things to do besides sitting around waiting for eighty to come along, so I don't think about that too much.

Has making money changed you?

> Well, with the Experience I really don't know how much we earn today. We just get enough money every week for what we need. I don't give a damn so long as I have enough to eat and to play what I want to play.

Is there anything you can't do?

> I can't express myself in conversation. I can't explain myself like this or that. So when we're on stage, that's all there is in the world. That's my whole life.

How far can you go with what you're playing?

> I don't know. You can go on until you bore yourself to death, I guess. I'm happy to be able to play like I feel now. I play it by ear, man! I know the audience is changeable, but I'm not afraid of tomorrow.

Where do your songs come from?

From the people, from the traffic, from everything out there. The whole world influences me. Everybody and everything is music. You don't plan songwriting. You don't get into a certain groove to write a song. You can get inspiration for a song any time, because music is just what you feel. The ideas come very easily. It's just getting the song together to where it's acceptable. I stay in bed most of the time or go to the park or somewhere. I write some of my best songs in bed, just laying there. I was laying there thinking of one when you came in. I dream a lot, and I put a lot of my dreams down as songs.

Do you dream in color?

Oh, definitely. The closest to a black and white dream I ever had was in pastel shades, you know? One time it was in pastel shades, and it was maroon, very light maroon, and then this big gold cliff out of the middle of nowhere. It was great! That was the closest I ever got to black and white.

What's your New Year's resolution?

To keep the axis turning so that love follows music as the night the day.

{IN JANUARY 1968, THE EXPERIENCE TOURED SWEDEN AND DENMARK.}

W E HAVE NEVER TRIED TO PLAY ANYTHING from *Axis* onstage before, so the Swedish public will be the first to experience that event. I've always liked Sweden, and I like to perform here because I feel the Swedish audience understands the purpose of our music. They've got so many different ways all over the world of showing appreciation, but Sweden is the one that shows appreciation more than anybody. They show it by being completely silent while you're playing – completely. I mean, there are a few rockers back there running around falling out of balconies. But the average person is completely quiet, and they wait until every last thing is over and then they clap.

Sounds like the walls caving in.

{JIMI WAS ARRESTED IN GOTHENBURG FOR SMASHING UP A HOTEL ROOM.}

We were going home when we met some friends who started a party. I drank quite a bit of schnapps. Then I don't remember anything. I think I woke up at the police station. I cut up my hand a little, and there were also a couple of things that got broken. It probably will be a while before my right hand is completely OK. It hurts like crazy, but the show must go on.

The newspapers made the thing seem bigger than it was. Do they always have to exaggerate? Everybody drinks some alcohol sometimes. It's only when famous people do that newspapers make headlines out of it. Nothing like that has ever happened to me before. I'm convinced somebody put something in my drinks. I'm sure about that, because the next day I didn't get a hangover, just a strange feeling I've never experienced before. From now on I'd better stick to tea and milk! Do you think there will be a lot of shit from this? I really feel bad about it. It'll be better next time, though. We're human beings too, just like anybody else, aren't we?

Since I made it to the top, everything has happened so fast. This pop business is so much harder than people think. It's nerve-racking and mind-bending. The people who dig ditches for a living don't know how lucky they are. We are constantly under pressure, and the workday is often twenty-four hours. Every show takes its pound of flesh. I can hardly get anything to eat. We're too much on the go. You see, even my skin is suffering from the lack of eating right. One often gets depressed. It's only natural that we need a stimulant sometimes. After Stockholm I'll take it easy for a while.

I need to slow down.

*   *   *   *

MOST OF ALL, I'D LIKE TO FORGET EVERYTHING BEFORE 1968. We call it the end of the beginning. It is now that I plan to start making real music. I want to create new sounds, try to transmit my dreams to the audience. Music must always continue to expand further out, further away. Kids listen with open minds, but I don't want to give them the same things all the time. It gets to be a bad scene coming out saying, "Now we'll play this song, and now we'll play that one." I want to keep doing fresh things, different songs, different things visually.

I'd like to experiment with different instrumentation – keep the basic trio but add other musicians temporarily when we want a different sound. I'm also trying to work out a whole new concept of putting on a show, something more in the form of a play with good stage presentation. Can you imagine taking *Othello* and putting it on in your own way? You'd write some real groovy songs. You wouldn't necessarily have to say the exact lines. Nobody would be the star. Everybody would be working together. Every single song would have a completely different and strange arrangement and setup. And we'd use films and stereo speakers in the back of the auditorium, all over the place. It's hard to explain, but it would be so natural, in a rehearsed way.

*   *   *   *   *   *

Above all, our records will become better, purely from the point of view of recording technique. We have not been happy with a single one. Our producer up till now, Chas Chandler, has not had the right feel when he turned the wheels in the control room. In the future we'll take care of that detail ourselves, together with Dave Mason, who has quit Traffic to spend time on this among other things.

We're cutting a new record between our tours. There'll be maybe two tracks from the new Bob Dylan album on it. In fact we've done one of them, *All Along The Watchtower*, already. Dylan goes his own way. Just at this time he is not very high in the music world, but he is taking his thing to the end. He is getting more and more of a songwriter. In *All Along The Watchtower* he said it so groovy.

I'm also looking forward to our six-week tour of the States, which starts in February.

BUT MOST OF ALL, RIGHT NOW I'M LOOKING FORWARD TO GOING BACK TO SLEEP...

sleep...

CHAPTER SIX
(February 1968–December 1968)

STONE FREE

EV'RY DAY IN THE WEEK
I'M IN A DIFFERENT CITY.
IF I STAY TOO LONG
THE PEOPLE TRY TO PULL ME DOWN.
THEY TALK ABOUT ME LIKE A DOG,
TALK ABOUT THE CLOTHES I WEAR,
BUT THEY DON'T REALIZE
THEY'RE THE ONES WHO'S SQUARE.

This is the second time we've been to the States. You can have a chocolate milkshake in a drugstore, chewing gum at gas stations and soup from little machines on the road. It's great, it's beautiful, it's all screwed up and nasty and prejudiced, and it has everything.

{FEBRUARY 1, 1968, THE EXPERIENCE'S FIRST AMERICAN HEADLINE TOUR OPENED AT THE FILLMORE WEST, SAN FRANCISCO.}

I DON'T EVEN REMEMBER THE FILLMORE LAST NIGHT. I feel completely out of my mind. It was like a scene. We were in the studio in London, into some groovy things, some really funky little things, and we were snatched out of the studio within a day of knowing nothing. Then we were thrown into the Paris scene, the Olympia theater, and we found ourselves waiting for two hours at London Airport. Then we found ourselves in New York, lost in the street. All these within hours of each other. Then they had a press conference, and here you are thinking about these songs. You have these songs in your mind. You want to hurry up and get back to the things you were doing in the studio, because that's the way you gear your mind.

Then we were thrown into the Fillmore. We wanted to play there, quite naturally, but you're thinking about all these tracks, which is a completely different thing from what you're doing now. If people only knew what state of mind we're in, like we're half there or not. We're constantly working, except when we sleep. Plus we don't get a chance to practice. Most of our practice is thinking about it. We've practiced about three times since we've been together. We just get a chance to jam sometimes, that's the only thing. The longest we ever play together is on stage.

But touring is one of those things you can't avoid. A lot of people don't have a full understanding of us yet, and if we stopped touring, they'd never understand. Nobody would hear us.

{THE EXPERIENCE WERE SCHEDULED TO PLAY AT THE CENTER ARENA, SEATTLE, ON FEBRUARY 12.}

I'm looking forward to going home. It's been seven years. Maybe I should call them and say, "Look, um, hey, I've started this group and ..."

I met my family, and we were happy for a change. There's my father, who's married again, and my brother, Leon, who's nineteen, I think, and is trying to form a band of his own now. And I've got a six-year-old sister, Genevieve, whom I'd never seen. That's how long I've been gone from home. She's a lovely little girl. She keeps every article she reads about me and all the pictures. I've got a picture of her. She's so cute. I'm very proud that I can send them articles from newspapers and send them money. That's the only way my father likes it. I told him, "Dad, I could buy you a home. I want to buy you a home this winter."

Before it all started happening nicely for us, I thought about the future. I thought, well, there's money to be made and I'm going to make it, but I'm not going crazy when it comes in. I saw so many cats in the music scene who'd made a lot of money and ended up twisted, rich but miserable, that I said, "I'm going to make it better organized for me if ever I get to that stage." Half the groups aren't free to change as they want to because they're all thinking about their career and thinking about their future so much. I don't really give a damn about my career or future. What I'm making money for is to make better things happen.

I WENT TO GARFIELD HIGH SCHOOL, my old school, where they kicked me out when I was just sixteen. I wonder if my old school teacher digs me getting the keys to Seattle? Maybe she's a Daughter of the Revolution now. Man, that Seattle thing is really something! The only keys I expected to see in that town were to the jailhouse. When I was a kid there I often nearly got caught by the cops. I was always gone on wearing hip clothes, and the only way to get them was through the back window of a clothing store. I did a concert for the kids there. Just me. I played with the school band in the gymnasium. Only thing wrong was that it was eight in the morning. They canceled first class to listen to me.

"Are there any questions? There must be somebody?"

How long have you been away from Seattle?

Oh, about five thousand years.

How do you write a song?

Right now, I'm going to say good-bye to you, and go out
the door and get into my limousine and go to the airport.
And when I go out the door, the assembly will be over, and
the bell will ring. *And as I get in the limousine and I hear the
bell ringing, I will probably write a song.*
Thank you very much.

✳   ✳   ✳   ✳   ✳   ✳   ✳

No city I've ever seen is as pretty as Seattle, all that water and
mountains. It was beautiful, but I couldn't live there. You get restless,
and before you know it you're too old and you haven't seen any of the
world. You've got this great big fat old world here, so who wants to
live in the same place forever? The next time I go to Seattle will be
in a pine box.

{THE TOUR CONTINUED ACROSS AMERICA THROUGH FEBRUARY, MARCH AND APRIL 1968.}

DIARY EXTRACTS:

February 25, Chicago. *After a while you remember the towns you been in by the chicks. We go into a new town and there's no time to do anything except some chick, so you can't help remembering the chicks. Except that lately I've been confusing the chicks and the towns and I've been taking pictures to remember them by.*

March 19. *Arrived in Ottawa. Beautiful hotel. Strange people. Talked with Joni Mitchell on the phone. I think I'll record her tonight with my excellent tape recorder – knock on wood – Hmm ... can't find any wood ... everything's plastic. Marvelous sound on first show. Good on second. Went down to a little club to see Joni. Fantastic girl with heaven words. We all go to a party. Millions of girls. Listen to tapes and smoked. Went back to hotel.*

March 20. *Left Ottawa city today. I kissed Joni Mitchell. Slept in the car awhile. Stopped at a highway diner – I mean a real one – like in the movies. Mitch and I discuss our plans for movie. Slight disagreement here and there but it will soon be straightened out. Nothing happened in Rochester tonight. Went to a very bad, bad, bad tasting restaurant. Thugs follow us. They probably was scared – couldn't figure us out. Me with my Indian hat and Mexican mustache, Mitch with his fairy-tale jacket and Noel with his leopard band hat and glasses and hair and accent. G'night all.*

March 21. *Today we play Rochester, N.Y. Really strange town ... Oh well. Two girls came up to my room by the names of Heidi and Barbara. Real groovy people. We played one show tonight. Very bad P.A ... bad hall ... patient people, but I kind of lost my temper with everything in general. Recorded show with tape recorder. After show we go to girl's house with party material. Someone outside got beat up by the hackers {motorcycle gang}. Stayed there over night in the tiger room. O.K.*

March 22. *Today we're in Hartford, Conn. I had a beautiful diary I kept while we were in Sweden – and of course I lost it. Hmmm ... I wonder what Catherina is doing now. I must call her soon, before she goes to Switzerland. She's the only thing I have to hold on to that's real. Better call her soon. Beautiful room I have. Bought more film, tape, etc.*

Just came back from the gig. Terrible! The people thought we were great. The stage manager dropped the power right in the middle of concert. So I am depressed. Gonna get completely smashed. Let's see ... where's that bottle ... Hmmm ...

March 23. *Well, we all rode through the most extreme weather today, from sunshine to blizzards and fog and everything. We're in Buffalo now. Played show. Great. Girls came around ... Oh no ... must think of Catherina and write my songs. Goodnight everyone.*

March 26. *I played Cleveland before, with Joey Dee. This tour's a merry-go-round. Tomorrow it's Muncie, Indiana, and then Someplace, Iowa.*

March 28. *We played in Cincinnati. I bought a new Jazzmaster here and a practice amp. Got the guitar for recording.*

March 29. WOW*! I'm stoned as hell in this hotel room with Mitch. The gig? Oh, yeah, groovy ...*

April. *We'll be late again, and Mitch still hasn't come down from his room. In the one and a half years that I've known him he's never been on time. Unpunctuality is a chronic sickness with him.*

✳   ✳   ✳   ✳   ✳   ✳   ✳

I LIKE THIS TOURING EXCEPT I DON'T LIKE THE TOURING, if you know what I mean. I dig doing shows in different towns, sure, but the hotels, the lack of service, the hang-ups when all you want is something simple to eat at the time you want to eat it. And you get no kind of private or personal life in this business. A person has to have five or ten minutes to himself every day. When you're resting after working for eighteen hours in a day and trying to have a quiet meal somewhere, there's always kids coming in and bugging you for autographs and pictures, or somebody looking at you really strange, whispering and all that. So, quite naturally, you get complexes about that. I can't have fun like anybody else.

And I get very bored on the road. I get bored with myself and the music sometimes. Like, what can you do on a tour? People scream for the "oldies but goodies." So you have to play the "oldies but goodies" instead of some of the things you want to get into.

Of course, those kids out there expect to hear the records we've cut. They've already heard the record, but still they want us to play the song like the record. We could either bring the whole box of tapes on stage, or they could go back home, set pictures of us up on the wall and listen to the record! In person we play things a different way. Two shows a night are tough, and we soon find ourselves completely boxed in with the same numbers. It really gets sticky and icky. So we usually start jamming onstage and have more fun doing that. That really gets it over. Sometimes a three-minute song might stretch into ten.

We play as we feel, and people will never get to know us by just listening to our records. We could never make enough to cover all our moods. It's only by seeing our shows when each performance is spontaneous and different that they will come to understand what we are all about.

{IN APRIL 1968, WHILE STILL ON TOUR, THE EXPERIENCE BEGAN RECORDING SESSIONS FOR *ELECTRIC LADYLAND* AT THE RECORD PLANT IN NEW YORK.}

In England, the studios don't have anything to work with compared to what they have here in America. Then they come out with the best sounding records and the most new sounds. Even the limitations are beautiful, because they make people really listen. The engineers have more imagination over there. They do some fantastic things, just like the way they fought World War II. It's all very positive, the atmosphere, the engineering, everything. When you're with an engineer over there you're with a human being. You're with someone who is doing his job.

Here in America, all an engineer does is his thing. He's a complete machine, just like the tape recorder he's working. You feel that the human being is missing, that the studio isn't interested in anything but the bill, the $123 an hour. There's no atmosphere, no anything. But that's only in some instances. At the Record Plant we have a good cat. He's on the ball. This is the first time we've recorded seriously here.

I WANTED TO MAKE *Electric Ladyland* a double LP, but it was a big hassle. The record producers and the companies don't want to do that. I'd be willing to spend every single penny on it if I thought it was good enough. Well, I'll do that, and then they'll leave me out there!

The reason I wanted this as a double LP is because we had so many good songs. I don't know if they're commercially good, but time was going by and our sound was changing and there were these songs you haven't ever heard. If you put out a single LP and then wait six months for another single, it's going to be out of style. We're trying to give as much of us from six months back to now as we can. Because we're constantly evolving.

Electric Ladyland is different from anything we've ever done before. It's slightly electric funk every once in a while, and it goes into the complete opposite on some songs, complete fantasy. There are other sides of you, and sometimes they leak out on the records too. Like you might tell them something kinda hard, but you don't want to be a completely hard character in their minds. That's where the fantasy songs come in.

People think you don't know what you're talking about, but it all depends on what the tracks before and after might have been. The record wasn't just slopped together. Every little thing you hear on there means something. I don't say it's great, but it's the Experience. It has a rough, hard feel on some of the tracks. It's part of us, another part of us.

I WANT TO SHOW YOU DIFFERENT EMOTIONS,
I WANT TO RIDE THROUGH
THE SOUNDS AND MOTIONS,
ELECTRIC WOMAN WAITS FOR YOU AND ME.

GOOD AND EVIL LAY SIDE BY SIDE
WHILE ELECTRIC LOVE PENETRATES THE SKY
I WANT TO SHOW YOU ...
I WANT TO SHOW YOU.

Some groupies know more about music than the guys. Some people call them groupies, but I prefer the term "Electric Ladies." My whole *Electric Ladyland* album is about them. It starts with a ninety-second sound painting of the heavens. It's typifying what happens when the gods make love – or whatever they spend their time on. I know it's the thing people will jump on to criticize, so we're putting it right at the beginning to get it over with.

The way I write things, they are just a clash between reality and fantasy. You have to use fantasy to show different sides of reality. It's not a little game that we're playing, trying to blow the public's mind and so forth. For instance, *1983* is something to keep your mind off what's happening today but not necessarily completely hiding away from it, like some people might do with certain drugs and so forth ...

Hooray, I awake from yesterday,

Alive, but the war is here to stay
So my love, Catherina, and me
Decide to take our last walk through the noise to the sea
Not to die but to be reborn
Away from lands so battered and torn
Forever, forever.

Oh say, can you see it's really such a mess,
Ev'ry inch of earth is a fighting nest
Giant pencil and lipstick tube-shaped things
Continue to rain and cause screamin' pain
And the Arctic stains from silver blue to bloody red,
As our feet find the sands and the sea
Is straight ahead, straight up ahead …

Well, it's too bad that our friends can't be with us today,
Well, it's too bad. **"The machine that we built would never save us,"** that's what they say.
That's why they ain't coming with us today.
They also said, **"It's impossible for a man to live and breathe underwater."**
Forever was their main complaint.
And they also threw this in my face, they said,
**"Anyway, you know good and well it would be beyond the will of God,
And the grace of the King,"** Grace of the King.

So my darling and I make love in the sand,
To salute the last moment ever on dry land.
Our machine, it has done its work, played its part well,
Without a scratch on our bodies we bid it farewell.
Starfish and giant forms greet us with a smile,
Before we go under we take a last look at the killing noise
Of the out of style, the out of style … out of style

So down and down and down and down and down and down we go,
Hurry, my darling, we mustn't be late for the show.
Neptune champion games to an aqua world is so very dear
"Right this way!" smiles a mermaid, I can hear Atlantis full of cheer,
Atlantis full of cheer, I can hear Atlantis full of cheer.

On some tracks you hear all this dash and bang and fanciness, but all we're doing is laying down the guitar tracks and then we echo here and there. We might have the drums or the guitar swing around to the other side with the echo going the opposite way – what you call "pan the echo."

We're using the same things anyone else would, but we use them with imagination and common sense. In *House Burning Down* we made the guitar sound like it's on fire. It's constantly changing a dimension, and up on top that lead guitar is cutting through everything. For the record's benefit we just try to take you somewhere – as far as the record can go.

On *Voodoo Chile* we just opened the studio up, and all our friends came down after jam sessions. Steve Winwood is on one track. Al Kooper is on another, but his piano is almost drowned out. It just happened that way, so the piano is there to be felt and not heard. A lot of my songs happen on the spur of the moment. I start with a few notes scribbled on some paper, and when we get to the studios the melody is worked out and lots of guys all kick in little sounds of their own. It's satisfying working this way. We don't want anything too carefully planned.

We did *Voodoo Chile–Slight Return* about three times because they wanted to film us in the studio. "Make it look like you're recording, boys," one of those scenes, you know.

So,

"Okay, let's play this in E. Now a-one and a-two and a-three," and then we went into it.

Except for *Watchtower* and *Burning Of The Midnight Lamp*, it was all recorded at Record Plant studios in New York. *Watchtower* comes from British sessions and was recorded as a single. It's our own arrangement. We used this solo guitar as different types of sounds, as slide, then wah-wah and then straight.

You just don't do everybody's songs, and if you're going to do them you don't necessarily have to copy them. Noel kicked in one of the songs. Mitch and he are singing this English rock type thing called *Little Miss Strange,* but mostly they're mine.

In the early days I used to ask my producer to drown my voice in the backing track, I thought it was so bad. But I was basing my assessment of my voice on the wrong things. Now I base my singing on real feelings and true thoughts.

I learnt that from listening to Dylan. Dylan has a lousy voice technically, but he's good because he sings things he believes in. True feelings are really the only qualities worth listening for in a voice.

I felt like *All Along The Watchtower* was something I had written but could never get together. I often feel like that about Dylan. Every time I perform his *Rolling Stone* it makes me feel so good, as though I had taken something off my mind.

{IN MAY 1968, WHILE STILL IN THE PROCESS OF RECORDING AND MIXING
ELECTRIC LADYLAND, THE EXPERIENCE FLEW TO ITALY FOR A SERIES OF EUROPEAN
CONCERT DATES.}

I'LL COME BACK TO ROME. I love this wonderful city. Tomorrow we end our Italian tour. Then I'll fly to New York for a day to sign a contract. In four days we'll be in Switzerland, then a vacation in Spain. We really need one, we're simply overtired. We can't continue at this pace for long. I feel we could end up has-beens sometimes. I feel it's happening now. I think people are getting tired of us. I've had all kinds of bad hallucinations. We come back from America, and people say, "Here are those three shaggy-haired guys again!"

{MOST OF JUNE 1968 WAS SPENT AT THE RECORD PLANT, FINISHING *ELECTRIC LADYLAND.* IT WAS MID-JULY BEFORE JIMI GOT A FEW DAYS VACATION IN SPAIN (MAJORCA). ON AUGUST 1 THE EXPERIENCE BEGAN ANOTHER TOUR OF AMERICA.}

*   *   *   *   *   *   *

DIARY EXTRACTS:

August 1. *Weather's beautiful here in New Orleans. Food's O.K. Everybody's on fire – but a groovy fire. Can you imagine, Southern police protecting ME? We could change America! The gig was actually great. Turned them on with physical music, come back to the hotel and get stoned and make love to "Pootsie," a TALL Southern blonde.*

August 2. *Well, back again and we are in the beginning of a change – San Antonio, TEXAS. Down the street about three blocks from this motel is the World's Fair. Hope I get a chance to see it.*

August 7. *In New York again. Linda was at Salvation in white and gold. She loves me. She is beautiful. She loves me. Tomorrow she will be gone again, but she never gets away.*

Mitch and Noel were quick in wanting to go back home from this tour. Our music is getting uglier, but so are the times. We aren't living in *Blue Danube* times now, are we? There's all this violent thing in the States right now. Playing the Midwest, like Cleveland or Chicago, is like being in a pressure cooker, waiting for the top to blow off. In New York it's very violent, actually. The music might sound loud and funky, but that's what's in the air right now, isn't it?

I dig playing in the South a little more than in the North. Texas is fine. I don't know why – maybe it's the weather. New Orleans is great, Arizona's fantastic. Utah? Well, once we're off stage it's another world, but the people are great. When we played at the gigs they were really listening, they were really tuned in some kind of way or another. So much depends on the audience.

{AUGUST 17, ATLANTA MUNICIPAL AUDITORIUM.}

I didn't really feel up to it this afternoon because we were pretty tired. Very, very tired as a matter of fact. We just got straight off the plane and came over here. We had free time for about half an hour. It's just like having a recess in school.

*The first show was a drag. It was a bore. The people were waiting for flames or something, and I was waiting to get through to those people in a music way. Who wants to sit in a plane eight days a week and come down and see people's faces saying, "*Are you going to burn your guitar tonight?*" What's that shit about?*

I get a kick out of playing. It's the best part of the whole thing. But then you come to things like people saying, "Well, you're supposed to be an entertainer, so you're supposed to be this to us, and we're buying your records and we're making you this and we're making you that." They think they have us for the rest of our lives. Who wants to go through all that? It's the public who can smash a group to pieces by the way they treat them. They squeeze something until it is completely dry.

The success is not good. It makes my work suffer. It's the reason *Electric Ladyland* is still not released yet. It was supposed to be out on July 21. Still, there is a difference between doing your own shows and getting the bread than going around the same sort of circuit with guys like Little Richard and King Curtis.

{SEPTEMBER 1, DENVER, COLORADO.}

We played out there at Red Rocks and I had a lot of fun. People are on top of you there. At least they can hear something. It's very hard sometimes if you know those people out there are not going to hear anything. That's how it should be, natural theater-type things, outside where a hundred thousand people can get together. The Grand Canyon or Central Park. I'd like for us to play outside more because the air does something to the sounds. It's terrible to have to rely on the Madison Square Gardens all the time, because those places are not for real good rock music. Then you have to go to the small clubs and get your ears blasted away. I think they should make special buildings for loud electronic music, like they make special buildings for restaurants and hotels.

{SEPTEMBER 7, VANCOUVER.}

My dad, brothers and sisters, my grandmother and her boyfriend and my cousins were out there tonight. I don't get a chance to see them until maybe we play here. This is only the second time in about eight years. I wanted to give my parents a new car, but I guess they didn't want it. I guess they're proud.

Each day on a tour like this kind of moves into the next. Nothing different about each one throughout a week. Sometimes I have this feeling I'm getting too mechanical. We've been playing *Purple Haze*, *The Wind Cries Mary*, *Hey Joe*, *Foxy Lady*, which I really think are groovy songs, but we've been playing all these songs for two years. I know we have to change some way, but I don't know how to do it. I suppose this staleness will finish us in the end.

The promoters think you're a money-making machine, and they have no faith in you. It's dog-eat-dog constantly. I can always tell the artificial people from the real music people, the ones who care about the music and what the musicians are doing. The trouble is, in this business there are so many artificial people. They see a fast buck and keep you at it until you are exhausted and so is the public, and then they move off to other things. That's why groups break up – they just get worn out. Musicians want to pull away after a time, or they get lost in the whirlpool.

I'm so tired I could drop, but I find the relaxation comes from thinking about music. Nothing else moves me. I hear music in my head all the time. Sometimes it makes my brain throb, and the room starts to turn. I feel I'm going mad. So I go to the clubs and get plastered. Man, I get real paralytic.

But it saves me ...

The jukebox dies, the lights go down
The sawdust floor has claimed the last of my drinks.
Intoxication makes my eyes a fool
And makes my brain almost cease to think.
Candlelight plays upon the ring upon my hand
Which doesn't seem like my hand anymore...
The bar is closed, I guess I'll go back
To my little red velvet room on the basement floor.

A car horn interrupts my staggering, my name is called,
my mind's up against a wall for a second or two.
Well, if it isn't my old friend, says a chuckle from within the ear.
I've been looking all over for you.
My memory beats and robs my smile and greetings
Don't reach this man I first gave in to quite a while ago.
A lot has changed and I still walk towards
The little red velvet room on the basement floor...

155

I don't really know if I have friends or not. I mean, the cats in the group and all this and Chas Chandler and Gerry Stickells, the road manager. Granny Goose, that's his nickname. My friends are the people who give me a belief in myself.

I spend most of my time just writing songs and so forth, and not making too much contact with people. They act just like the pigs that run these places, these countries. They base everything on the status thing. That's why there's people starving, because humans haven't got their priorities right.

I get mad when I hear about people dying in wars or ghettos. Sometimes I'd like to say **fuck to the world,** but I just can't say it because it's not in my nature. And I can't let it show, because it's not really a good influence on anybody else. People just make me so uptight sometimes. They don't give me inspiration, except bad inspiration to write songs like *Crosstown Traffic*, because that's the way they put themselves in front of me, the way they present themselves.

I got better things on th

You jump in front of my car when you know all the time
Ninety miles an hour, girl, is the speed I drive.
You tell me it's alright, you don't mind a little pain,
You say you just want me to take you for a drive.
You're just like crosstown traffic,
So hard to get through to you, crosstown traffic
I don't need to run over you, crosstown traffic,
All you do is slow me down,
And I'm tryin' to get on the other side of town.

I'm not the only soul who's accused of hit and run
Tire tracks all across your back,
I can see you had your fun!
But darling, can't you see my signals turn
from green to red,
And with you I can see a traffic jam straight up ahead.
You're just like crosstown traffic
So hard to get through to you, crosstown traffic,
All you do is slow me down,
And I got better things
on the other side of town.

I like to treat people fair until they screw you around. You can be terribly honest these days, but this tends to bring out a certain evil thing in people. My eyes are very bad, and sometimes I go into a club and I might not see somebody and they might get all funny – "Oh, you're big-time now, you won't talk to me!" And I say, "Hello. I was thinking about something. I'm sorry." Because you daydream a lot.

I don't think I'm difficult. I get a little deep at times and don't talk, but that's because I'm thinking about my music. I've got notes in my mind, so I can't kill them by talking. People get the wrong idea. They think I am being ignorant. I'm not, but after a while, I must admit, I don't care what they think.

I guess I could do without people. In fact, sometimes I'd rather be alone. I like to think. Yes, gee, man, I'm a thinker. I can really get lost thinking about my music. But then I think so much I have to get out among people again.

{October 5, Honolulu.}

*Hawaii is the place. I had some beautiful days there. So many girls.
I smashed my car up at 100 miles per hour in a 50 miles per hour zone.
I got hurt real bad, and my face got scratched. I've been just freaking
out for a few months.*

{October 10–12, concerts and recording at Winterland, San Francisco.}

*It was great. We'll use one or two of the things, maybe three of them.
But I was out of tune a few times. With the way I play the guitar it
might jump out of tune, and so I have to take away 30 percent of
my playing for three or four seconds to get back in tune. You might not
even notice it.*

You can usually tell how a show will go about halfway through
the first number. Naturally, you try to play a little better when you
get good feelings from an audience. But if there's no response at all,
it doesn't bother me too much. I try to turn them on regardless.
When the audience is quiet while you're playing, that's really great.
That means they're listening. There's a few little piggies in the back
row squealing every once in a while, but I don't think about those
things. I think about the feeling that is there. It's like all the spirits
collect for an hour and a half. That's the way it's supposed to be. It
doesn't call for talking and yelling, does it?

{JIMI SPENT THE REST OF OCTOBER 1968 AT T.T.G. INC. SUNSET-HIGHLAND RECORDING STUDIOS, HOLLYWOOD, CALIFORNIA. IN NOVEMBER HE MOVED BACK TO NEW YORK FOR A SERIES OF EAST COAST CONCERTS.}

RIGHT NOW, WHEN IT COMES TO ACTUAL PLAYING, I like to do really funky clubs. Nice sweaty, smoky, funky, dirty, gritty clubs. Because you can really get to the people then. All this stuff where you stand two thousand miles away from the people, I just don't get any feeling at all.

What you can do in America, especially New York, is meet up with guys and just go out and jam somewhere. Jamming is the thing now because everybody wants to create some music. The club scene is so informal. Things don't have to be official all the time. You just go in, wait your turn and get up there and blow. It's like a workhouse. It's nice to sweat.

I remember we used to play sometimes when even the amplifiers and guitars were actually sweating. It seemed like the more it got sweaty, the funkier it got and the groovier.

Everybody melted together, I guess!

The sound was kickin' 'em all in the chest.

I dig that!

Water and electricity!

That's what being a musician's about.

That's what you live for.

160

Half the people don't know how to jam nowadays. They don't play together, they don't really think about the other person. That's what jamming is about, it's playing with everybody. It's kind of like making love to one another musically or like painting a picture together. After playing a while you feel the flow that goes through the music, like changes of key, timing and breaks. Finally you get where you can be more together than on a record you've worked on for two weeks. It can be one of the most beautiful things if you have time to hit it.

We have a certain little crowd, which is great. We've all been through the teeny-bopper group scene. There will still be a need for good performance groups, but this scene is developing along the lines of jazz, where cats from different bands always jam together. We are like a band of gypsies who can roam free and do what we like. We are trying to produce real music and to hell with the imaginary thing.

Maybe the group only exists for one album, maybe they go on for a year or so together, but they don't stretch it out once it has started losing the sheer exuberance of jamming together. Like they take up a kind of sound and then develop it, and out goes the heart of it. It becomes a sort of exercise in technique. Everybody loses interest, and back they go to a more basic thing. Blues is basic. So too is a lot of country music. So you get these two things there at the roots of what's going on.

We are not breaking up – **no, no, no!** There are so many rumors going round right now. We are discussed over and over. There has been too much talk about how I can go it alone. But I would never have made it as the Jimi Hendrix Experience without Noel and Mitch. I've always insisted we were a three-piece group and should be acknowledged as such. Our group is just going to be called "Experience" in the future. It's wrong that the spotlight should just be turned on one guy all the time.

What we need now is a good rest. We've hardly had a day off since the group was formed two years ago. None of us has had time to sit down and think by himself. We might be working a little less, but our records will be better, because we'll have better peace of mind.

You know, it's like being married with me and Mitch and Noel. Sometimes they might want to tell me something and I might not be able to understand, and it gets frustrating. Anytime you make a song, you want your own personal thing in it as well as the group's. So we'll continue to play together, but we have to make sure that each one of us has a chance to grow within the group. All three of us have individual interests. We work together in the Experience, but we are not tied down to that alone.

I'd like to see Mitch and Noel getting into the things that make them happy. Doing your own thing is what it's all about. Noel has this thing called Fat Mattress and wants to go on an English rock thing. How about that! Anglo Rock! A pseudo blues-rock music! Mitch is involved in his Elvin Jones thing. He's becoming a little monster on the drums. He's the one I worry about losing. He's becoming so heavy behind me that he frightens me!

Oh, I'll be around, don't worry ... doing this and that. I'm not going solo, I'm just going to be a little different. I want to do a Super Group album with guests like Clapton, Winwood and Mayall. People I really dig. But we'll still keep on with the Experience. We're together as long as we want to be.

* * * * *

Room Full of Mirrors
Soliloquy

THIS ROOM IS REALLY BEYOND MY IMAGINATION. THIS ROOM IS FULL OF MIRRORS. THERE'S NO DOOR, NO WINDOWS, NOT EVEN A CARPET AS OF WHERE I COULD VOMIT OUT MY OTHER THOUGHTS. TOP, BOTTOM, LEFT, RIGHT, FRONT, BEHIND ME, I CAN SEE NOTHING EXCEPT FOR THIS ROOM SET IN A MIRROR. AND WITH THIS ROOM BEING NOTHING BUT MIRRORS, I CAN PROBABLY STAY IN IT.

THERE'S A CERTAIN PERSON THAT COMES IN HERE CERTAIN TIMES, AND HE LOOKS SOMETHING LIKE ME. REALLY STRANGE. I DON'T EVEN KNOW HIM, AND HE BRINGS HIS FRIENDS IN, AND HE BRINGS MY WHOLE WORLD, MY WHOLE DAY AND NIGHTS IN. HE CHANGES MILLIONS OF TIMES, HE TURNS ROUND ON A CIRCLE AND DRIVES ME COMPLETELY OUT OF MY MIND. THERE ARE VERY, VERY INTERESTING THINGS THAT HE TELLS ME. HE SAYS I AM HIM AND HE IS ME, AND HE SAYS, "MAN, YOU REALLY ARE IN NEED, AND YOU JUST SCREAM, BUT YOUR VOICE IS NOT HIGH ENOUGH TO SCREAM WHAT YOU WANT TO SCREAM." I SAY, "MAN, DIG, WHAT DO I WANT TO SCREAM?" AND AS I SAY THIS THE MIRRORS ARE BEATING THE HELL OUT OF MY MIND. I FEEL LIKE MY MIND IS HUNG UP ON A CLOTHES RACK. WHERE'S MY LOVE? MY LOVE COMES INTO MY IMAGINATION, NOT TO MY EYES, BUT I CAN'T SEE MY LOVE. I WANT TO SO DESPERATELY.

I WANT TO GRASP ON TO ANYTHING BESIDES MYSELF. I TURN TO THE WORLD. WHAT HAS THE WORLD TO OFFER ME EXCEPT PATS ON THE BACK, SHAKING HANDS, MAKING PLANS? HE SAYS, "YOU BETTER TURN THAT RECORD OVER. TAKE ALL SOUNDS OUT OF YOUR HEAD. YOU BETTER SCREAM FOR SOME KIND OF RELEASE." I SAY, "MAN, DIG, I'VE BEEN SCREAMIN'. I SCREAM RAYS OF ACID, I SCREAM RAYS OF SPEED, I SCREAM RAYS OF TEA, COFFEE, MILK, CIGARETTES. WHAT ELSE? WHAT ELSE?" HE SAYS, "LET ME SEE YOUR FRIENDS. SCREAM OUT THE REFLECTION OF YOUR FRIENDS." AND YOU KNOW I'M GONNA SCREAM. THERE ARE A MILLION LIONS TRAPPED IN THE GRAND CANYON. SCREAM OUT. FRIEND. GOD, TELL THIS IDIOT TO GET THE HELL OUT OF ME. "MAN," HE SAYS, "SCREAM YOUR LOVE AGAIN." AND I SCREAM AS HARD AS HELL. LOVE! SAY SOMETHING. EVEN IF YOU ARE NOTHING AT ALL, JUST HELP ME, FOR I FEEL RIGHT NOW THAT I AM LESS THAN THAT. I HEAR ANOTHER VOICE COMING THROUGH THE MIRROR TO THE FRONT, AND I SNATCH AND BREAK, SMASH IN FRUSTRATION. SOMEBODY HELP ME. SOMEBODY PLEASE HELP ME! SO HE SAYS, "START ALL OVER AGAIN." I START ALL OVER AGAIN. MAN, I CAN'T EVEN TELL MY FEET FROM THE SAWDUST ON THE FLOOR. I can see through that.

Yeah, brother, I can see that.

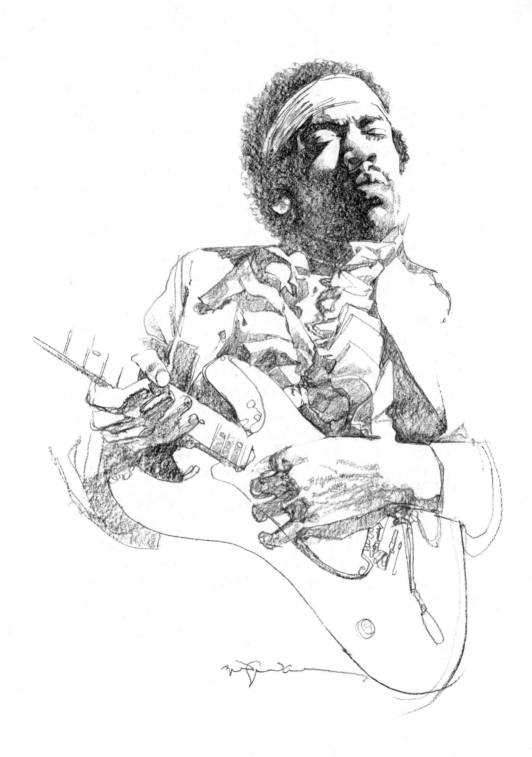

CHAPTER SEVEN

(January 1969–June 1969)

ALL ALONG THE WATCHTOWER

A MUSICIAN, IF HE'S A MESSENGER, IS LIKE A CHILD
WHO HASN'T BEEN HANDLED TOO MANY
TIMES BY MAN, HASN'T HAD TOO MANY
FINGERPRINTS ACROSS HIS BRAIN.
THAT'S WHY MUSIC IS SO MUCH HEAVIER
THAN ANYTHING YOU EVER FELT.

Dear Sirs,

Here are the pictures we would like for you to use anywhere on the LP cover. We would like to make an apology for taking so very long to send this, but we have been working very hard indeed, doing shows AND recording. And please send the pictures back to Jimi Hendrix Personal & Private, c/o Jeffrey & Chandler, 27 East 37th St., NY, NY, after you finish with them. Please, if you can, find a nice place and lettering for the few words I wrote named ... 'Letter to a Room Full of Mirrors' on the LP cover. The sketch on the other page is a rough idea of course ... but please use ALL the pictures and the words. Any other drastic change from these directions would not be appropriate according to the music and our group's present stage — and the music is most important. And we have enough personal problems without having to worry about this simple yet effective layout.

Thank you.

Jimi Hendrix

{ELECTRIC LADYLAND HAD BEEN RELEASED IN THE U.S. IN OCTOBER 1968. IT WAS IN THE CHARTS FOR THIRTY-SEVEN WEEKS AND REACHED #1, THE ONLY EXPERIENCE ALBUM TO ACHIEVE TOP BILLING.}

I 'M KIND OF PROUD of *Electric Ladyland* because I really took the bulk of it through from beginning to end on my own, so I can't deny that it represents exactly what I was feeling at the time of production. It was really expensive to produce, about sixty thousand dollars, I guess, because we were on tour at the same time, which is a whole lot of strain on you. It's very hard jumping from the studio onto the plane, doing the gig and then jumping right back into the studio.

We were having to always go back in the studio again and redo what we might have done two nights ago. We wanted a particular sound. We produced it and mixed it and all that mess, but when it came time for them to press it, quite naturally they screwed up, because they didn't know what we wanted.

There's a 3-D sound being used on there that you can't even appreciate because they didn't want to cut it properly. They thought it was out of phase. See, when you cut the master, if you want a really deep sound, you must almost remix it again right there at the cutting place, and 99 percent don't do this. They just say, "Oh yeah, turn it up there, make sure the needle doesn't go over there, make sure it doesn't go under."

We didn't get a chance to complete it because we were on tour again. When I heard the end result I thought some of the mix came out kind of muddy. Not exactly muddy, but kind of bassy. Then the engineers retaped the whole original tape before they pressed the record for Britain, so much of the sound that existed on the American album was lost. Now I'm learning more about this kind of thing so that I can handle it myself.

I care so much about my work. I record stuff I believe is great. The only time I get uneasy is when I know that the pop critics and writers are waiting for me to fail so they can jump all over me. This is how pop is. You have a hit record and, gee, they love you, but you have one failure and they kill you.

It's like a tightrope.

THE NEW ALBUM, *Electric Ladyland,* seems to have got me into a bit more trouble with people. It seems that folks in Britain are kicking against the English cover. Man, I don't blame them. I had no idea they had pictures of dozens of nude girls on it. I wouldn't have put that picture on the sleeve myself, but it wasn't my decision.

Over here there's just a picture of me and the boys. First I wanted to get this beautiful woman, Veruschka. She's about six-foot-seven, and so sexy you just want to, *hmmm* ... We wanted to have her leading us across the desert and have these chains on us. But we couldn't find a desert because we were working, and we couldn't get hold of her because she was in Rome. Then we had this one photo of us sitting on *Alice In Wonderland,* a bronze statue in Central Park, and we got some kids and all.

I didn't know a thing about the English sleeve. Still, you know me, I dug it anyway. Except I think it's sad the way the photographer made the girls look ugly. Some of them are nice looking chicks, but the photographer distorted the photograph with a fish-eye lens or something. That's mean. It made the girls look bad. But it's not my fault. It's the other folks, you know, the people who are dying off slowly but surely. Anybody as evil as that dies one day or another.

I've got a lot to offer pop, but pop has less to offer me back because it is run by people who only talk about what is commercial. All these record companies, they want singles, because they think they can make more money. But you don't just sit there and say, "Let's make a single." We're not going to do that. I consider us more musicians, more in the minds of musicians. You'll have a whole planned-out LP, and all of a sudden they'll make, for instance, *Crosstown Traffic* a single. See, *Electric Ladyland* was in a certain way of thinking, and the sides were played in order for certain reasons. It's almost like a sin for them to take out something in the middle to represent us at that particular time. They always take out the wrong ones. It shows you how some people in America are still not where it's at.

You don't even have no friend scenes. I walked into a store and saw this record with my name on it. When I played it I discovered that it had been recorded during a jam session I did in New York when I was a backing musician with a group called Curtis Knight and the Squires. We had only been practicing in the studio, and I had no idea it was being recorded.

That album was made from bits of tape, tiny little confetti bits of tape. Somebody has taken their scissors from Sears and Roebuck and spliced a few seconds of tape and put it on there. It's a whole lot of hogwash. I'm only on about two tracks. I didn't sing on *Hush Now*. That was dubbed on later by Knight trying to copy my voice. On the other, *Flashing*, all I do is play a couple of notes, and the guitar was out of tune, and I was stoned out of my mind.

Man, I was shocked when I heard it. It was just a jam session, and here they just try to connive and cheat and use. It's a really bad scene. Somebody trying to capitalize on somebody's name. They never told me they were going to release that crap. That cat and I used to be friends. That's the real drag about it.

{JANUARY 4, 1969, THE EXPERIENCE APPEARED ON THE LULU SHOW ON BBC TV. JIMI UPSET LULU AND THE BBC BY ABRUPTLY SWITCHING FROM *HEY JOE* INTO *SUNSHINE OF YOUR LOVE* AS A DEDICATION TO THE RECENTLY DISBANDED CREAM.}

It was the same old thing with people telling us what to do. They wanted to make us play *Hey Joe.* I was uptight about it, so I caught Noel's and Mitch's attention, and we went into *Sunshine Of Your Love.* If you play live, nobody can stop you or dictate what you play, beyond setting a time limit. I dream about having our own show.

Say, wouldn't it be great to take over the studio like they do in Cuba!

We'd call it *The Jimi Hendrix Show — Or Else!*

And there will be no smoking in the gas chamber while we're on!

We're planning to promote our own concerts at the Royal Albert Hall on February 18 and 24. We'll do two shows ourselves and book some nice groups. We'd like Jim Capaldi's new band and Spike Milligan. We'd like him to be the compere. He's my sort of comedian. They don't have *The Goon Show* in America. They're masterpieces. Those are classics. They're the funniest things I've ever heard, beside Pinky Lee. Remember Pinky Lee? They are like a whole lot of Pinky Lees together. Just flop them out together. I used to be a Pinky Lee fan. I used to wear white socks.

{FOR THE REST OF JANUARY THE EXPERIENCE TOURED EUROPE, PLAYING IN SWEDEN, DENMARK, GERMANY, FRANCE AND AUSTRIA.}

It's nice to be back in Stockholm. I like Sweden. I wanted to give everything to get them into my music, but I failed. We haven't played in so long that it takes a while to get into the groove of it. It made me desperate. The worst of it was the staring, lifeless faces in the front row.

We also played in Gothenburg, and many people wondered if it didn't feel a little unpleasant to play there after the trouble with the broken window at the hotel last year. We stayed at another hotel this time.

I think pop groups have a right to their own private life. People should judge them by what they do onstage, as singers and musicians. Their private life is their own business, and people shouldn't know too much about that. You can't expect artists to be goody-goodies all the time. In any case, kids aren't as dumb and easily influenced as some people think. They have a lot of common sense. Any kid that does something bad because a certain pop idol did it would probably have done it anyway.

✳ ✳ ✳ ✳ ✳ ✳ ✳

LETTER FROM JIMI HENDRIX TO HIS MANAGER'S OFFICE, WEDNESDAY, FEBRUARY 5, 1969:

Most of these notes are in preference to a hopeful contact with England via phone ... The date of February 10th meet must be canceled because of exhausting but very important business over here ... If 24th Albert Hall England goes through confirmed we should, as you said, either abandon or really rethink the idea of the three individual groups idea for 24th and stress in England phone call that if by all means possible we should have previous day of concert (AH England) for ultimate private rehearsal in preparations for recording. Maybe afternoon, evening, whatever available ...

Tables: trash everything out of Generation that we do not need. This done as soon as possible.

At least let it be mentioned, interview with Rolling Stone *will not be over telephone but in person... Preferably tape interview. Matter of fact, please ask me about things like interviews in immediate future and please keep in mind that tape interviews are a must if it's a major or important article. We have an offer from* Village Other *(weekly newspaper, very good) about interview. Please have them call if possible to set a date before I leave or call them.*

Recording: Albert Hall February 18th & 24th? Please try to find out definitely about who will engineer recordings. Very important As Soon As Possible. Please tell Mercury Records to stop hassling over names and payment agreements as far as Buddy Miles Express album goes. Please tell them both the group, the Emmy and myself are quite happy with the idea.

I would like to see personal accounts on expenses (as close as possible) to the present. Also on personal rough net figures. I know they should be able to take at least 5 or 10 minutes today and reply over the phone or by messenger service in an envelope an estimate of what is happening ...

For replacing time and acts on the bill 24th please look into booking Jethro Tull, Noel Redding's outfit (if not only for 20 minutes). A very definite word from Noel about that. We would like to try recording the Albert Hall on the 24th as well as the 18th. 24th possible: Jethro Tull, Cat Mother or Buddy Miles Express or "Face" (check with Speakeasy's Roy Flynn).

Later this evening I would like to check out moneys we may have coming in or lined up like posters, publishing royalties, record royalties, writer's, etc.

Oh yes, almost forgot: please make it clear to Mercury (contracts included or whatever legal means) that in due time the Buddy Miles Express new LP will be one of the biggest for Mercury and we are all (the group and myself) working very hard on it and it would seem to be honestly fair for my name alone to appear as producer and receive normal producer's fee. If there are hang-ups on Ann Tanzy's (sp.?) side of the fence as far as whose name goes where, she may very well be represented on the LP as supervisor. I know a name on an LP jacket sounds like a small tut, rather an ego thing, but one of my ambitions is to be a good producer and extend. Therefore that's one of the main themes in the idea of the name being there. I plan to finish to the bone the whole LP as long as the necessary papers and attitudes on both sides (Mercury and us) are together. If I could work with Buddy and group without being entirely hung up over this fact — over those fat starving sick hicks, about them wanting something for nothing — and to keep Ann in her proper place. I could most certainly write songs with Buddy ... and that side is where I'm inching toward ... percentage from writer's royalties for sure.

Jimi Hendrix

{THE ROYAL ALBERT HALL CONCERTS ON FEBRUARY 18 AND 24, 1969, WERE THE EXPERIENCE'S LAST PERFORMANCES IN ENGLAND.}

I feel so relaxed now at concerts. Our music is in a very solid state – not technically, just in the sense that we can feel around the music and get into things better. The communication is lovely. If I'm out of tune I just stop and get in tune. That's the way I like it to be. It's not a Flash Gordon show, everything all neat and rehearsed.

I don't read music, and it's hard for me to remember any riffs because I'm constantly trying to create other things. That's why I make a lot of mistakes. These days everybody seems to be busy showing what polished performers they are, and that means nothing. People are getting so much wiser. They don't want to hear about this manufactured, tinfoil music. They want to hear the best in the field. I was talking to some little kids, the people they call teenyboppers, and I said, "What are your favorite groups?" They said, "We like the Cweam, we like y'alls group." Beautiful. You know, their minds are different.

A COUPLE OF YEARS AGO all I wanted out of life was to be heard. Now I'm trying to figure out the wisest way to be heard. I don't want to be a clown anymore. I don't want to be a rock and roll star. I'm just a musician. That is why we play more now and move around less. We don't break things up too much anymore. We haven't burned any guitars lately.

Those little things were just added on, like frosting, but the crowd started to want them more than the music. The more the press would play it up, the more the audience would want it, the more we'd shy away from it. Do you see where all that fits? You can't prostitute your own thing. You can't do that.

Half of the things I did because I just felt like it at the time. I'd say, "Maybe I should smash a guitar or something tonight," and they'd say, "Yeah, that'll be cool." So I worked up enough anger so I could do it. It was fun! Maybe everybody should have a room where they can get rid of all their inhibitions. My room was a stage. But you can only freak out when you feel like it. I used to feel like it a lot, but not anymore. You'd have a heart attack if you were doing it every night like I was. I'd be dead by this time!

I feel very guilty when people say I'm the greatest guitarist around. What's good or bad doesn't matter to me. It's how you feel about what you're doing that matters. If only people would take a more true view and think in terms of feeling. Your name doesn't mean a damn. It's your talent and feeling that matter. I just toss off those people who are doing it for their own egotistic scene instead of trying to show off another side of music.

We'd like to turn everyone on to all we know. You can always sing about love and different situations of love, but now we're trying to give solutions to all the protests and the arguments that they're having in the world today. Every time we come into town everybody always looks towards us for some kind of answer to what's happening to them, which is a good feeling, but it's very hard. Therefore I have to live the life, I have to witness all these bad scenes and all these good scenes, so then I can say what I found out. Anybody can protest, but not too many people can offer a decent answer. So we're going to try and do that.

Have you missed London?

It's great to be in London again. This is the place I feel most comfortable, and I feel the English are my friends. The English girls are just too much. I was out walking yesterday and it must have been about five degrees below zero, but they were still walking around in their little miniskirts. Yes, we missed London.

How do you like living in Handel's home?

I didn't even know this was his pad, man, until after I got in.

There's a cherub with a broken arm on the ceiling ...

That's the groovy thing about him. He can fly with a broken arm.

Do you have feelings for classical music?

Oh yeah, it's beautiful, it's very beautiful. I like Handel and Bach. It's like a homework type of thing. You can't hear it with friends all the time. You have to hear some things by yourself. See, different music is supposed to be used in different ways. I believe the best time to listen to classical music is any time when it's very quiet or your mind is very relaxed. When you feel like daydreaming, maybe ...

Do you like classical rock?

To each his own. In another life the people who are trying to do it may have been Beethoven or one of those cats. But this is a rock and roll era, so the people get into rock. Every era has its own music.

What about jazz?

If I go to somebody else's place and hear somebody else's records, then I'd listen to jazz. But if I'm at home I'd never put on a jazz disc. I consider jazz to be a lot of horns and one of those top-speed bass lines. If it's axes, I like to listen to it. But to play it – I don't think that way. I like free-form jazz, like Charlie Mingus and this other cat who plays all the horns, Roland Kirk. The groovy stuff instead of the old-time hits, like when they get up and play *How High The Moon* for hours and hours. But I don't happen to know much about jazz. I know that most of those cats are playing nothing but blues though – I know that much!

Didn't you play with Roland Kirk recently?

I had a jam with him at Ronnie Scott's, and I really got off. It was great. I was so scared! It's really funny. I mean, Roland, that cat gets all those sounds. I might just hit one note and it might be interfering, but we got along great I thought. He told me I should have turned it up or something. We have different moods, and I think some are on the same level that Roland Kirk is doing. If people read this they'll say, "That guy must be joking," but I really think we are doing the same things. I really want to cut an album with Roland Kirk. He's the most beautiful human being alive that plays jazz. He hasn't really even started yet. When you hear him you can hear so much of the future. You can hear some of the things he's going to go into. I mean, not necessarily by notes, but you can hear it by feelings. Running through a field, an everlasting field of beautiful things, man.

How do you see the future of pop music?

I don't know. I'm not a critic, you know. And I don't like the word "pop." All it means to me is Pilgrimage of Peace.

How would you like your music to be described then?

We are trying to play real music. We don't play blues, although some people seem to think we do. Rather we play a mix of blues, jazz, rock and roll and a lot of noise. We call our music Electric Church Music because it's like a religion to us. I don't like the name "church" because it sounds too funky, too sweaty – you think of a person praying between his legs on the ground – but until we find something better we'll have to use that.

An Italian critic recently called you the Paganini of the guitar.

Paganini? Who's that? Oh, the greatest violin artist of all time. That makes me extremely happy.

Does success make you happy?

All the things I thought were important before I had a hit record are just as important now. Trying to understand people and respect their feelings, regardless of your position or theirs. The beautiful things are still the same, the sunset and the dew on the grass. No material wealth changes the way I think about these things. If you're looking for real happiness, you go back to the happiest days you had as a child. Remember when playing in the rain was fun?

Has success changed you?

It depends on what you think is success. Success, to me, is doing your utmost, achieving the ultimate. Well, I have not done that. I don't consider myself even started yet. I always try to get better and better, but as long as I'm playing I don't think I'll ever reach the point where I'm satisfied. I think I shall always be looking for success.

You have received the highest critical acclaim.

That's part of the establishment's game. They're trying to blow us all up and give us awards so that they can just dust us away. But we're not here to collect awards. We're here to turn people on to the right way because there are some really strange scenes coming through.

Are you going to play more concerts in England?

We plan to have the Albert Hall our last job for a while. I wish we could play more places around the country because I dig England, and when we play here it is a big thing for us. But the problem is we are doing more recording now, and we have to do an American tour in April and May.

Is there any truth in the rumors about you retiring?

You know, when you're young, most people have a little burning thing, but then you get your law degree and go into your little cellophane cage. You can do the family thing. I've wanted to do that at times. I've wanted to go into the hills sometimes, but I stayed. Some people are meant to stay and carry messages.

THERE'S OTHER MOVES I HAVE TO MAKE NOW, a little more towards a spiritual level, through music. We concentrate mostly on sound. It's a very hard and harsh and primitive sound, not necessarily good or bad or stoned. You get the feeling that you're going to get something out of it if you let your mind flow with it. It's more than music. It's like church, like a foundation for the lost or potentially lost.

That's why the kids don't mind when you take fifteen minutes setting up for a concert. Guys come out and set up instruments, and they turn their backs to the audience, taking time to get ready. The kids like it ... it's like watching something being born. They become like fathers to the music.

We're making our music into a new kind of bible, a bible you carry in your hearts, one that will give you a physical feeling. We play unbelievably loud. Not piercing loud – it's another type of loudness that goes through your chest.

There's so many tight-lipped ideas and laws around, and people put themselves in uniform so tightly that it's almost impossible to break out. Subconsciously, what all these people are doing is killing off all those little flashes they have.

We try to make our music so loose and hard-hitting that it hits your soul hard enough to make it open. It's like shock therapy or a can opener. You hypnotize people to where they go right back to their natural state, which is pure positive – like in childhood when you get natural highs. And when they come down off this natural high, they see clearer, feel different things. It's all spiritual. Except when the eardrums come in!

Everything is electrified nowadays, so therefore the belief comes through electricity to the people. That's why the name "Electric Church" flashes in and out. If you say you are playing Electric Church Music, people go "Gasp, gasp!" or "Exclaim, exclaim!"

The word "church" is too identified with religion. A lot of kids don't find nothing in church.

I WAS SENT TO CHURCH WHEN I WAS A KID, and I remember when I got thrown out because I had improper clothes on. I had tennis shoes and a suit, and they said, "Well, that's not proper." We didn't have no money to get anything else, so I just got thrown out of church anyway. It's nothing but an institution, so they're not going to find NOTHING there.

Don't get me wrong, I'm not trying to stop people going to church, but as long as I'm not hurting anybody else I don't see why they should tell me how to live and what to do.

I suppose human beings have to believe in something. People feel they have to be directed in some way, have to have something to follow, regardless of whether it's true or not.

The only thing I believe in now is music. Music is going to break the way because music is in a spiritual thing of its own. It's like the waves of the ocean. You can't just cut out the perfect wave and take it home with you. It's constantly moving all the time. Music and motion are all part of the race of man. It's the biggest thing electrifying the earth. Our music is just as spiritual as going to church. We want it to be respected as such. Our scene is to try and wash people's souls.

I SEE FINGERS, HANDS AND SHADES OF FACES
    REACHING UP BUT NOT QUITE TOUCHING
    THE PROMISED LAND.
I HEAR PLEAS AND PRAYERS AND
    DESPERATE WHISPERS SAYING,
    OH LORD, PLEASE GIVE US A HELPING HAND.

Quite naturally things are going bad here, but the idea is to get your own self together. You have to live with peace of mind, and that has to be found within yourself. I think everybody should believe in himself. I suppose, in a way, that's also believing in God. If there is a God and He made you, then believing in yourself is also believing in Him. Once you carry God inside yourself, then you're part of Him. That doesn't mean you've got to believe in Heaven and Hell and all that stuff, but it does mean that what you are and what you do is your religion. When I get up on stage and sing, that's my whole life.

That's my religion.

I am Electric Religion.

         *   *   *   *   *

MY GUITAR IS MY MEDIUM, and I want to turn the world on. Music flows from the air. That's why I can connect with a spirit. There's no telling how many lives your spirit will go through, die and be reborn. Like my mind will be back in the days when I was a flying horse. Before I can remember anything, I can remember music, stars and planets. I could go to sleep and write fifteen symphonies.

My personal philosophy is my music. It's almost all philosophy in a very hazy form, because it's still part of a progression. It's just like a little baby, and it hasn't even reached the stage for it to walk by itself. Music is my whole life. There is nothing but music and life – that's all. They flow together so closely, it's sort of like a parallel. And that's the effect I would like my music to have on the audience – if not an awakened state, then maybe in a hypnotic state.

The everyday mud world we're living in today compared to the spiritual world is like a parasite compared to the ocean. One way to approach the spiritual side is facing the truth. If only people wouldn't concentrate on the superficial things they might find the real meaning and true happiness. That's why the world's screwed up today, because people base things too much on what they see, and not on what they feel.

STARTING AT ZERO

{IN APRIL AND JUNE 1969, THE EXPERIENCE, NOW THE HIGHEST PAID TOURING BAND IN THE WORLD, WENT ON ANOTHER MAJOR TOUR OF AMERICA.}

There was a time when I worried about money. I worried about whether I was getting all I was entitled to. I wanted to get money to hold me together, to do what I want to do in life. I wanted to make money so I'll have somewhere to live when I get bald, you know, when all these little curls fall out, when all this shit falls out.

Everybody wishes for more money. But people get so greedy with money that they choke themselves. They don't want to give it up, and that makes it nothing but a drug, just like anything else. As a matter of fact it's one of the worst drugs.

That's why I'm glad I just smoke!

I travel most places without any money, actually. I like to witness different types of life, rich and poor. If I starve tomorrow, it would just be another experience to me. I'd still give money away to people if they needed it badly. What's money except a piece of paper? Just like a marriage license.

Sometimes it gets to be really easy to sing the blues when you're supposed to be making all this money. Because money is getting to be out of hand now. Too many musicians nowadays think of the money and the image first, before they figure out what they're trying to get across. They get a chance to make all this money, and they say, "Wow, this is fantastic!" and they lose themselves, they forget about the other half of themselves. So therefore you can sing a whole lot of blues. Sometimes the more money you make, the more blues you can sing.

The money scene can turn you into a slave to the public, a zombie, a penguin. Who wants to be a big, lifeless pop idol anyway? This is where the kids get more distracted than the musicians actually, with the fame and imagery and all that stuff. It's like a circus that might come in town. **"Oh wow! Watch that,"** you know? And then they see you fade away, and they go and feed upon the next thing.

The music's better now, and people don't even know. It's right in their faces, and they don't even know how to accept it, because they have to have gimmicks and imagery to go by. That's what made me cut my hair off, because of this being a slave to the public. I cut it short to protest.

{DURING THIS TOUR, MEMBERS OF THE BLACK PANTHERS MADE APPROACHES TO JIMI.}

They asked us to give benefit concerts for the Black Panthers, which I was really very happy for them to do. I was honored and all this, but we haven't done it yet. Mike Jeffery is taking care of that side of things, so I don't know if we ever will. I just want to do what I'm doing without getting involved in racial or political matters. I know I'm lucky that I can do that, because lots of people can't. In the U.S. you have to take a stand. Either you're a rebel or you're a Frank Sinatra type.

When I was younger I wrote protest songs that were bitter. I don't now, because there's a lot of political things happening out there that I really have to get away from, or I'd find myself in too much of a box situation. If I had anything to say, I'd have to say it to everyone. And I'd have to get really involved before I could say anything.

I don't feel involved. I feel almost completely lost now, sometimes from almost everything. I feel sorry for the minorities, but I don't feel part of one. I'm for the masses and the underdog, but not for just trying to get the underdog to do this or that, because I tried before and got screwed so madly millions of times. So now I'm just for anybody who can do the job.

RACE ISN'T A PROBLEM IN MY WORLD. I don't look at things in terms of races. I look at things in terms of people. I'm not thinking about black people or white people. I'm thinking about the obsolete and the new. There's no color part now, there's no black and white. The frustrations and riots going on today are all about more personal things. Everybody has wars within themselves, so they form different things, and it comes out as a war against other people. They get justified as they justify others in their attempts to get personal freedom. That's all it is.

It isn't that I'm not relating to the Black Panthers. I naturally feel a part of what they're doing, in certain respects. Somebody has to make a move, and we're the ones hurting most as far as peace of mind and living are concerned. But I'm not for the aggression or violence or whatever you want to call it. I'm not for guerrilla warfare. Not frustrated things like throwing little cocktail bottles here and there or breaking up a store window. That's nothing. Especially in your own neighborhood.

✳   ✳   ✳   ✳   ✳   ✳

I don't feel hate for anybody, because that's nothing but taking two steps back. You have to relax and wait to go by the psychological feeling. Other people have no legs or no eyesight or have fought in wars. You should feel sorry for them and think what part of their personality they have lost. It's good when you start adding up universal thoughts. It's good for that second. If you start thinking negative it switches to bitterness, aggression, hatred. All those are things that we have to wipe away from the face of the earth before we can live in harmony. And the other people have to realize this too, or else they're going to be fighting for the rest of their lives.

I hope at least to give the ones struggling courage through my songs. I experience different things, go through the hang-ups myself, and what I find out I try to pass on to other people through music, so it won't be so hard for them. There's this song I'm writing now that's dedicated to the Black Panthers, not pertaining to race, but to the symbolism of what's happening today. They should only be a symbol to the establishment's eyes. It should only be a legendary thing.

BLACK IS GOLD IS PURE
AND THE TRUE KINGS OF THIS EARTH,
SO I SAY IT'S UP TO US TO STRAIGHTEN OUT THIS MESS.
WE GOT TO GO THROUGH HELL, AND THEN
THAT'S THE LAST OF THIS MISERABLE TEST.

BUT THE SUN KNOWS, AS THE WIND BLOWS,
AND THE FIRE GROWS
TOWARDS THE FAR SHORES, AND THE WATER FOAMS,
TO MAKE STEAMED BONES OF ALL THOSE
WHO DON'T BELIEVE
THAT BLACK IS GOLD IS THE KINGS OF THIS WORLD.

LET'S PRAY WE ALL AGREE,
WE'VE GOT TO STRAIGHTEN OUT THE FAMILY TREE.
LIFE IS FOR YOU AND ME TOGETHER,
THAT'S THE WAY IT WAS MEANT TO BE.
WHITE MAN, WATCH YOUR MOUTH,
BECAUSE OUR DRUMS THEY FACE THE SOUTH.

YOU BETTER ADJUST YOUR PLACE IN THIS WORLD
BEFORE YOUR HAIR IT STARTS TO CURL,
AND THE YELLOW, RED, AND BLACK OF THIS WORLD
WILL TEAR YOUR ASS AND SOUL APART.

STARTING AT ZERO

{ON MAY 3, 1969, THE EXPERIENCE arrived in CANADA FOR A PERFORMANCE AT TORONTO'S MAPLE LEAF GARDENS. ALTHOUGH EVERYONE HAD BEEN WARNED TO TAKE EXTRA CARE BECAUSE OF TORONTO'S REPUTATION FOR STRICT CUSTOMS CHECKS, A JAR CONTAINING PACKETS OF HEROIN AND A METAL TUBE STAINED WITH HASH RESIN WERE FOUND IN JIMI'S FLIGHT BAG.}

I'm innocent, completely innocent. It must have been a frame, or it was just a very bad scene, because it ain't anything it was. I really don't see how anyone can put a needle into themselves. I had pneumonia when I was young, and I used to scream every time they put that needle in me.

Anyway, half the people don't know what drugs and everything are nowadays. You've got winos and drunkards out in the streets begging for money, and nobody seems to care about this. Some people will kill for a few cents to buy a drink. Matter of fact, they have big picnics where you can carry your cans of beer, go out there and get stoned sloppy drunk. And your mind is completely numb, and you don't think of nothing but how stoned you are.

One thing I am sure of, it's wrong to classify all drugs under one heading. Pot is completely different from hard drugs. And smoking marijuana is way better than drinking. As a matter of fact, it's helped a lot of people. I think smoking pot will probably be legalized in five or ten years. This is just the beginning of the cold war between those who want pot and those who don't. It seems to me to be silly to be sent to jail for smoking a natural plant. They should carry out a big inquiry into the effects of pot, just to see how harmful it really is.

There's a lot of drugs that slipped into the music scene from the simple fact that a lot of musicians think different than other people, they live different than other people, so therefore they have different releases than other people. But everybody can't dig it, because some people's minds just aren't that way. It's nice for the people who have minds for it.

It could be entertainment for some people and something really groovy for somebody else. And I think some of the drug scene seeped in through the music because everybody wants their own identification in some way or form. Some people believe they have to go into LSD or what-have-you to get into the music. I have no opinions about that at all. Different strokes for different folks, that's all I can say.

THIS I REALLY BELIEVE, that anybody should be able to think or do what they want as long as it doesn't hurt anybody else. It's your own private thing if you use drugs of any kind. It's nobody else's concern. Drugs are, in general, a very hip and mysterious experience. I just used them for a certain thing, as a step towards seeing it both ways, if you like. All Indians have different ways of stimulation – their own steps towards God, spiritual forms or whatever.

The trouble starts when people let it rule them, instead of using it as a step to something else. I see a lot of people who just sit around and get stoned. It's up to them not to make it into an escape.

{JIMI WAS GRANTED BAIL AND A HEARING WAS SET FOR DECEMBER 8, 1969. THE EXPERIENCE WERE ALLOWED TO GIVE THEIR PERFORMANCE AT MAPLE LEAF GARDENS, AND THE TOUR CONTINUED ON TO NEW YORK, THEN CHARLOTTE, NORTH CAROLINA. ON JUNE 20, THEY GAVE AN UNEVEN PERFORMANCE AT THE NEWPORT POP FESTIVAL.}

I've been having kind of a hard time over it all. People are starting to take us for granted, abuse us. It's that "what-cornflakes-for-breakfast?" scene. Pop slavery, really. I feel we're in danger of becoming the American version of Dave Dee, Dozy, Mick and Tich.

Sometimes, no matter how badly you play, people come up to you and say you were fantastic, and that really hurts, especially when you are trying to progress. That's too much burden on me. It hurts me inside, because you know the truth in yourself and sometimes people don't really try to understand.

We've been working solidly for about three years. It's the physical and emotional toll I have to think of. You go somewhere, the show is a bit under what it should be and you are told you are slipping. But it's the strain. It's the strain of the moral obligation to keep going, even when you don't feel that you can manage even one more show.

I'm as human as anybody else, and it's impossible for me to work on and on without ever needing to take a break and forget and rest for a while. After this tour is over I'm going to take a long vacation, maybe in Morocco or Sweden or way out in the Southern California hills.

Maybe I'll never get to take that break. All I know is that I'm thinking about it most of the time now, and that doesn't help create the right mood. Because I get very bored, regardless of how good anybody else is. And I'm sure other people get bored too. It's like I get bored with myself. I just can't play guitar anymore the way I want to. Sometimes I get very frustrated on stage, and I think it's because it's only three pieces. It restricts everybody – Noel and Mitch, too. But then again, I think that even if there were a thousand people in this group it still wouldn't be enough.

{ON JUNE 29, 1969, THE EXPERIENCE PERFORMED FOR THE LAST TIME TOGETHER AT THE MILE HIGH STADIUM, DENVER. THE THREE-DAY ROCK FESTIVAL ENDED AMID RIOTS AND TEAR GAS.}

"We see some tear gas.
That's the start of the Third World War,
so pick your sides now. Besides a lot of tear gas in the air, suppose they put us in the air. Yeah, let's make up our minds to make our own world here tonight . . .
Hmm, I wish I was out there with you.
This is the last time we're playing in the States, and like, it's been really a lot of fun. Noel Redding has his thing together called the Fat Mattress, we'll be looking out for them. Mitch Mitchell has a thing together called Mind Octopus.
Like to say, here's for all the Americans who really feel proud to be Americans. **But we're talking about the new Americans, OK?** *Let's stand up for that."*

{AFTER THE CONCERT, NOEL REDDING ANNOUNCED HE WAS LEAVING THE EXPERIENCE.}

Noel Redding is into more harmonic things, when you sing and so forth, and he went to England to get his own group together. He probably has reasons in the back of his mind, so I'm not going to down that. Noel and I are still friends, but he has his own ideas, and musically I want to go somewhere else. Plus I want to get into more of an earthier bass player.

I'm not sure how I feel about the Experience now. I died a thousand times in this group and was born again. But after a while you have to get yourself straightened out. Maybe we could have gone on, but what would have been the point of that, what would it have been good for? It's a ghost now, it's dead, like back pages in a diary. I'm into new things, and I want to think about tomorrow, not yesterday.

CHAPTER EIGHT
(July 1969–January 1970)

EARTH BLUES

I SEE MYSELF GETTING THROUGH ALL
THE DRASTIC CHANGES,
GETTING INTO BETTER THINGS.
I LIKE TO CONSIDER MYSELF
TIMELESS.
AFTER ALL, IT'S NOT HOW LONG
YOU'VE BEEN AROUND
OR HOW OLD YOU ARE
THAT MATTERS,
IT'S HOW MANY MILES
YOU'VE TRAVELED.

{IN JULY 1969, JIMI RENTED A HOUSE OUTSIDE THE VILLAGE OF SHOKAN IN UPSTATE
NEW YORK, MOVING IN WITH BILLY COX AND OTHERS.}

I FIRST MET BILLY COX when we were in the U.S. Airborne. We used to pinch parachutes. We used to play together, and since then he's been gigging around Nashville and California. Billy plays more of a solid bass, and we're doing a lot of guitar and bass unison things, nothing but a lot of rhythms and patterns. We're starting to really make good contact with each other because we realize how important a friend is in this world.

I'M FINDING OUT THAT IT'S NOT SO EASY,
'SPECIALLY WHEN YOUR ONLY FRIEND
TALKS, LOOKS, SEES AND FEELS LIKE YOU,
AND YOU DO THE SAME JUST LIKE HIM.

With the Experience there was more room for ego-tripping. All I had to blast off stage were a drummer and the bass. But now I want to step back and let other things come forward. We're going to take some time off and go out somewhere in the hills and woodshed, or whatever you call it, until I get some new songs and new arrangements, so we'll have something new to offer. The new thing will consist of writers too. We have this family thing we're trying to get together, but it's best not to harp upon us, the personalities and all that. The body of the music itself is what counts.

That's where we go from.

We're going to play mostly outside. It'll be like a sky church sort of thing. You can get all your answers through music, and the best place is through open air. We're going to play a lot of places, like in the ghettos, in Harlem and so forth. Free when we can.

{JIMI'S NEW BAND MADE ITS DEBUT AT THE WOODSTOCK MUSIC AND ARTS FESTIVAL ON AUGUST 18, 1969.}

"I see that we meet again, mmm!
Dig, we'd like to get something straight.
We got tired of Experience and every once in a while we was
blowing our minds too much, so we decided to change the whole thing
around and call it Gypsy Sun and Rainbows.
For short it's nothing but a Band of Gypsys.
We have Billy Cox from Nashville, Tennessee, playing bass,
we have Larry Lee playing guitar – Yellin' Lee!
And Juma and Jerry Velez on congas.
And we have a heart, Granny Goose, excuse me,
Mitch Mitchell on drums.
Yours truly on meat whistle."

Strangely, there were only fifteen thousand people left when we played. I insisted on playing in daylight, which meant waiting until the fourth day, and most of the kids had split by then. I don't know what all the fuss was about the National Anthem. I'm American, so I played it. They made me sing it in school, so it was a flashback, and that was about it. All I did was play it. I thought it was beautiful, but then, there you go ...

I dug the Woodstock Festival, especially Sly Stone. I like his beat, I like his pulse. Richie Havens is outasight – and the guy from Ten Years After. I was just a little bit jealous when I saw him play. A festival of five hundred thousand people was a very beautiful turnout. I hope we have more of them. The nonviolence, the very true brand of music, the acceptance of the crowd, how they'd had to sleep in the mud and rain and get hassled by this and that. There's so many scores you can add up on this thing. If you added them all up, you'd feel like a king.

I'd like everybody to see this type of festival, see how everybody mixes together in harmony and communication. But anybody can get a field and put a lot of kids in there and put on band after band. I don't particularly like the idea of groups after groups. It all starts merging together. It's like the money thing of it. Everybody wants to get on the bandwagon. They don't give a damn about those kids out there. If it rains, well, it rains.

500,000 halos ... OUTSHINED
THE MUD AND HISTORY.
WE WASHED AND DRANK IN GOD'S TEARS OF JOY,
AND FOR ONCE ... AND FOR EVERYONE ...
THE TRUTH WAS NOT A MYSTERY.

WE CAME TOGETHER ... DANCED WITH
THE PEARLS OF RAINY WEATHER.
RIDING THE WAVES OF MUSIC AND SPACE,
MUSIC IS MAGIC ... MAGIC IS LIFE ...

If parents want to love their kids they should be aware of their music. Music has so much to do with what is happening today. People have to realize that. It's better than politics. They look up to us quicker than they'll look up to what the president says. That's why you had a lot of people at Woodstock.

TALK TO THE PARENTS, the so-called other generation, because they have a way of overprotecting their young, of putting them in boxes. They put themselves in boxes too, and that's not a right way of living. Younger people, their minds are a little keener and they can figure this out, and since they can't get release and respect from the older people, they go into these other things, and their music gets louder and it gets rebellious. It's just that they're trying to find their own identification. They're tired of joining the street gangs, they're tired of joining militant groups, they're tired of hearing the president gab his gums away. They want to find different directions. They know they're on the right track, but where in the hell is it coming from?

The flower scene was an experiment. Now it's just a fashionable clique. Flower power will not get you up a hill if you run out of gas, will it? Why make a big issue out of it? The scene now is like bells and everything, and all those pseudo hippies running around flashing their little "Love not War" badges. Those kind won't last because they're going to hop onto the next train, any train that comes close to them and is easy to hop.

I don't like classifications, regardless of the scene. Why put yourself in a category when you can start your own little groove happening? You have to be a freak in order to be different, and those freaks are very prejudiced. You have to talk in a certain way in order to be with them, and in order to be with the others you have to wear your hair short and wear a tie. We shouldn't have to keep carrying the same old burdens around. So we're trying to make a third world happen ...

AND YOU LOOK OUT OF YOUR WINDOW
　　AT THE NOISE AND CRAZY BUSTLE OF LIFE —
IT IS NOT SCREAMING FOR TODAY, IT IS NOT MADE FOR TODAY.
　　AND THE VISIONS OF EARTH'S TEARS,
　　　　THE RIVERS OF FUTURES BEING BORN.

{AFTER THE WOODSTOCK FESTIVAL, JIMI TOOK HIS NEW BAND INTO THE RECORDING
STUDIO, THE HIT FACTORY IN NEW YORK.}

There's a lot of groups that are trying to keep harmony amongst the people. I've seen Crosby, Stills and Nash burnin' ass. They're groovy. Western Sky Music, all delicate and ding-a-ding-ding. I like the Impressions. I like that touch. I like that flavor. It's like an enchanted thing if it's done properly. I almost cry sometimes when I hear Otis Redding's stuff. You get that real good feeling, and then you get lumps in your throat, and shit — yeah, that's when the stuff is poppin'. If they keep on going I know I'm going to be embarrassed, because I know I'm going to cry.

See, these are classical composers. These are the people that need to be really, really respected. They give the people good-time music so they can release their frustrations and so forth, like black and white standing next to each other with hammers ready to hit each other. People really have to start learning the value of things as they're living today. That's what's going to pull America out.

Music is a universal language, and if it were respected properly it would have a way to reach people. There should be no barriers. I think it should be brought outside — almost like the evangelists.

The other music should stay in clubs. They should just stay in their pretentious bag in clubs and cabarets and all that. There's only certain groups trying to get across a harmony message anyway. And we're one of them . . .

{ON SEPTEMBER 5, 1969, JIMI GAVE A FREE CONCERT AT THE HARLEM STREET FAIR IN NEW YORK.}

This whole thing is under the benefit of United Block Association, and we hope to do more gigs for them. I think more groups that are supposed to be considered heavy groups should contribute to this cause. As a matter of fact, what we're trying to stress is that music should be done outside in a festival type of way, because a lot of kids from the ghetto, or whatever you want to call it, don't have enough money to travel across country to see these different festivals. They don't even have the six dollars to go to Madison Square Garden.

I always wanted a more open and integrated sound, and it bothers me that some black people can't get into our music. But they are so hung up about other things. Sometimes when I come up to Harlem people look at my music and say, "Is that white or black?" I say, "What are you trying to dissect it for? Try to go by the feeling of it." People are too hung up on musical categories. They won't listen to something because it sounds completely alien.

I wanted to release a special cut of *House Burning Down* for the R&B stations. We're not played on R&B stations because we haven't been exposed in this area as much as we have in others.

It's like, if a colored actress wants to make it in Hollywood she has to be ten times as good, so we have to be ten times as good for the soul people to even notice us. Not fakey good, I mean actually, naturally good.

Color just doesn't make any difference. Really, some people seem to think from their kneecaps! Look at Elvis. He could sing the blues, and he's white. He used to sing better when he sang the blues than when he started singing that "beach party" stuff. And look at the Bloomfield band, which is ridiculously outasight, and they really, really feel what they are doing, regardless of what color their eyes or armpits might be.

One time I said, "OK, let's go, we got this white cat down in the Village, man, playing harmonica really funky."

So we all go down the Village and hear Paul Butterfield, and **WOW,** WOW! It turned me on so much.

He was really deep into it. Nobody could touch him there, because he was in his own little scene and he was so happy. I always say let the best man win, whether you are black, white or purple.

Black kids think our music is white now, which it isn't. They say, "He plays white rock for white people. What's he doing here?" It just happens that the white people can dig it all of a sudden because some of them are very freaky and have imagination as far as different sounds are concerned. But the black kids don't have a chance too much to listen. They're too busy trying to get their own selves together. I want to show them that music is universal, that there is no white rock or black rock. There are only two kinds of music – **good and bad.**

{OTHER THAN AN APPEARANCE AT THE SALVATION CLUB IN NEW YORK ON
SEPTEMBER 10, 1969, JIMI GAVE NO PUBLIC PERFORMANCES FOR THE REST OF THE
YEAR. HE SPENT MOST OF THE TIME RECORDING AT THE RECORD PLANT.}

I've been going through a lot of changes in the last two years.
That's why I haven't released anything for a while. I'm very
inconsistent, you know. It all depends on how I feel. There are no
certain patterns I go by. Sometimes I write in a rush, but the things
I'm writing now take a little longer to say.

I'll tell you the truth. I heard *Are You Experienced?* recently, and it
seemed like I must have been high or something. I thought, "Damn,
I wonder where my head was at when I said all those things." Ha, ha!
The mad scientist! Honest to God's truth, I didn't know what I was
writing about then. I don't consider it the invention of psychedelic
music. It was just asking a lot of questions.

Albums are nothing but personal diaries. When you hear
somebody making music, they are baring a naked part of their soul
to you, and *Are You Experienced?* was one of the most direct albums
I've done. What it was saying was "Let me through the wall, man. I
want you to dig it." But later, when I got into other things, people
couldn't understand the changes. The trouble is, I'm schizophrenic
in at least twelve different ways, and people can't get used to it.

There's so many things I want to say and so little time that I get
almost like a frustrated old maid. That's why I go into these different
moods, and I'm sometimes very temperamental. I can't help it. I don't
think I'll ever get the chance to do all the things I really want to do as
far as music is concerned. But I can't stop thinking about music. It's in
my mind every second of the day. I can't fight it, so I groove with it.

I'VE BEEN WORKING HARD ON MY NEXT ALBUM. It will be called *Shine On Earth, Shine On* or *Gypsy Sun*. We have about forty songs in the works, about half of them completed. A lot of it comprises jams, all spiritual stuff, very earthy. I am having a string section and the Mormon Tabernacle Choir. It's going to give a lot of people the answers to questions they are searching for. It's going to straighten a lot of people out.

There's a great need for harmony between man and Earth. I think we are really screwing up that harmony by dumping garbage in the sea and air pollution and all that stuff. It's not just a fad, it's very serious.

They talk about some kind of earthquake. Dig! Where all the earthquakes stem from is bad vibrations! They get very heavy sometimes. Some of the vibrations people claim they are getting now are true, considering the fact that the earth will be going through a physical change soon. The solar system is going through a change, and it's going to affect the earth itself in about 30 years from now. Since the people are part of Earth, they are going to feel it too. In many ways they are a lot of the reason for causing it. This room is just a crumb from the crust of the pie, and there's no moving from any one land to another to save yourself.

Do not ignore the SUN ... for the sun is the truth shining to be seen.

I HAVE LIVED HERE BEFORE THE DAYS OF ICE,
AND OF COURSE THIS IS WHY I AM SO CONCERNED.
AND I COME BACK TO FIND THE STARS MISPLACED
AND THE SMELL OF A WORLD THAT HAS BURNED.

207

We must prepare for the amazing way that the truth will be presented. What's sometimes more amazing is how people miss the warnings of tidal waves, volcanoes, earthquakes, etc. I know inside they pretend to miss the message. We really don't seem to care for our children. How can you push it off when eventually, in the long run, we shall be our own children?

EVEN THE SUN IS HESITANT
  TO SHINE
THROUGH SLAG-FILLED CLOUDS
THAT COME FROM CROWDS
OF FACTORIES COUGHING
  WASTE, GRIT
    AND GRIME.

THE AIR COULD BE CLEARER BUT,
    DEAR ME,
WHO WOULD DARE THINK OF ALL
    THAT MONEY TO SPEND,
BLESS ITS LITTLE PAPER HEART,

    JUST TO KEEP FROM
BREATHING FILTH AND
  GASEOUS SLIME?

{TOWARD THE END OF 1969, NUMEROUS PROBLEMS WERE BUILDING UP IN JIMI'S LIFE: A LAWSUIT OVER AN OLD CONTRACT WITH PPX ENTERPRISES; FAILURE TO DELIVER A NEW ALBUM TO WARNER BROS. FOR OVER A YEAR; FINANCIAL PROBLEMS DUE TO THE BUILDING OF ELECTRIC LADY STUDIOS; AND PRESSURE FROM HIS MANAGEMENT TO KEEP ON TOURING.}

I don't know what's happening. I'm so exhausted, you know. I get destroyed by all these press conferences, by all unnecessary disturbing things. I have no time for my music. I just want to relax and think about myself and my music for a while. I want to bring my guitar, walk onstage and play, and then vanish, away from questions and people.

I haven't had time off by myself since I've been in this scene. I couldn't even save up some money and go to the hills because there's always problems, always hang-ups. I am very tired. Not physically. Mentally. My head's in a position now where I have to take a rest, or else I'll completely crack up pretty soon, in the next few hours or days. Seems like a – what do you call those things? Nervous breakdown. I've had about three of them since I've been in this business.

When you first make it the demands on you are very great. For some people they are just too heavy. You can sit back, fat and satisfied, or you can run away from it, which is what I did. I don't try to live up to anything anymore. If I'm free, it's because I'm always running.

I tend to feel like a victim of public opinion. They want to know about these girls, kicking people in the ass, doing the power to the people sign. I cut my hair, and they say, "Why'd you cut your hair, Jimi?" It was breaking up. They say, "Where'd you get those socks? What made you wear blue socks today?"

Then I started asking myself questions. Did I take too much solo? Should I have said thank you to that girl? Maybe I should grow my hair back. It's something to hide behind.

I GET STONED AND I CAN'T GO HOME,
BUT I'M CALLING LONG DISTANCE
                    ON A PUBLIC SAXOPHONE.
    MY HEAD IS DIZZY AND SHAKEN,
FEEL LIKE I GOT RUN OVER BY PUBLIC OPINION
                          AND THE PAST.

I can't help isolating myself from the world. Sometimes I just want to be left alone. Most people would like to retire and just disappear from the scene, which I'd LOVE to do, but then there's still things I'd like to say. There's so much rubbish going on by. I wish it wasn't so important to me. I wish I could just turn my mind off, you know, forget about the scene. But I worry about my music. You worry about anything you've built your whole life around.

I'm here to communicate. That's my reason for being around, it's what it's all about. I want to turn people on and let them know what's happening. Even if they have nine-to-five jobs and come back to the TV, that's what counts, to keep turned on.

{ANOTHER PRESSURE ON JIMI WAS THE IMPENDING TRIAL FOR DRUG POSSESSION IN CANADA. CONVICTION COULD MEAN UP TO SEVEN YEARS IN JAIL.}

{ON NOVEMBER 11, 1969, JIMI RECEIVED A LETTER FROM HIS ATTORNEY HENRY STEINGARTEN.}

Dear Jimi,

I was disappointed that you did not show up yesterday for our meeting. I tried to get you at the hotel but you were out. There are several things we have to straighten out and soon. These are as follows: 1. The Toronto case is scheduled for trial on Dec. 1st. We are all to meet at the Royal York Hotel in Toronto the evening of Nov. 29th. We will spend the following day with O. Driscoll preparing the case. Sharon Lawrence, Leslie Perrin, Bob Levine, Mike Jeffery and possibly Chas Chandler will all be there. I want to talk to you about this before we all go up to Toronto.

It may be of interest to you that Mark Stein's case for possession of narcotics was tried on Oct. 24th in Montreal and he was acquitted. His was a more difficult case than yours. In your absence yesterday I signed an agreement with Warner Bros. whereby if you fail for a period of three months to deliver an album to them as required under your contract, they may mix one from your reels. There are two albums now due. One for Capitol and the other for Warner. The editor is subject to your approval as is the album itself, and you have the right to substitute from material which you find unsuitable, but all this is under a tight schedule.

The legal expenses are rapidly becoming enormous ... The damage to the Woodstock house you rented came to $5,000 which also has to be paid. We do not have the money at this time to meet your obligations, and a good part of what you will be receiving from Warner and Sealark will go to meet these expenses. I have repeatedly tried to get you to understand the serious situation in which you find yourself and to urge you to cut down on your spending. I must repeat this is vitally necessary and I should like to take some of the money and invest it for you so that it is not available for immediate spending ...

DECEMBER 8, 1969, JIMI RETURNED TO
CANADA FOR HIS COURT CASE.

JUDGE:
What use could this aluminum tube have?

JIMI:
Probably a peashooter. I really don't know
what it is. Someone must have put it
in my bag.

JUDGE:
Do your fans ever give you drugs?

JIMI:
All the time.

JUDGE:
Are you saying you've given up drugs
entirely?

JIMI:
I've outgrown it.

JIMI WAS ACQUITTED ON ALL CHARGES.

I FEEL GOOD, HAPPY AS HELL. Canada has given me the best Christmas present I ever had. Man, it's a real game. But just don't blow it. Don't blow it. The Canadian government was just doing its job. To each his own. Sometimes people are too sensitive, as I was. Look what could have happened to me, even when I don't use drugs anymore. It's true, it's true! I don't take as much. That's what I was trying to tell them.

Quite naturally, people don't really need drugs. There are other things that you can actually benefit from. You know my song, *I Don't Live Today – Maybe Tomorrow*? That's where it's at. Things were getting too pretentious, too complicated. People were singing about acid itself! Things start to rule you. Images, drugs. Everybody forgets what happened to God. The soul must rule, not drugs. You should rule yourself and give God a chance.

The drug scene was opening up things in people's minds, giving them things that they just couldn't handle. The term "blowing someone's mind" is valid. People like you to blow their minds. Well, music can do that. You don't need any drugs. Music is a safe type of high. It's more the way it's supposed to be. That's where highness came from anyway, I guess. It's nothing but rhythm and motion.

Once you have some type of rhythm it can get hypnotic.

If you keep repeating it over and over again, most people will fall off after about a minute. You do that,

say for three or four or even five minutes, if you can stand it,

and then it releases a certain thing inside of a person's head. So, all of a sudden, you can bring the rhythm down a little bit,

and then say what you want to say *right into that little gap.*

As long as you want to believe the world is a stage,
      Then appoint me your electric stagehand ...
And I shall produce upon you an
              Overwhelming hurricane
      And sling you through to the vast middle
And let your body there tremble — but force to stand.
The middle, as calm as an untouched baby's brain.
      I shall let it drain away your clammy nerve
   And take my finger and scrape
           Around the edge of the bowl
And in your subconscious ear I shall serve it.
    And what you will witness will not be
              From my limbs direct
But by proxy, straight from your own script ...
Are you satisfied or do you want to stay the limit?

What's happening is that there's a sixth sense coming in. Everybody has their own name for it, but I call it "Free Soul." That's why everything is beyond the eyes now. You have to know how to develop other things that will carry you further and more clearly. They say the speed of light is the fastest thing – that's the eyes – but then there's the speed of thought, which is beyond that. For instance, you can get on the other side of this theme in a matter of thinking about it. That's why music is magic.

You can listen to anything that turns you on, anything that takes you for a ride. You have to ride with something.

People want to be taken somewhere.

I always like to take people on trips.

When I'm playing, man,
I go up in a rocket ship.
Don't know where I'm going to go,
but you can all come with me, every one of you if you want.

Join me on my ship.

IT'S VERY FAR AWAY,
IT TAKES ABOUT HALF A DAY TO GET THERE,
IF WE TRAVEL BY MY ... DRAGONFLY.
NO, IT'S NOT IN SPAIN, BUT ALL THE SAME,
YOU KNOW IT'S A GROOVY NAME,
AND THE WIND'S JUST RIGHT ...

HANG ON, MY DARLING,
HANG ON IF YOU WANNA GO.
YOU KNOW IT'S A REALLY GROOVY PLACE,
WITH JUST A LITTLE BIT OF SPANISH CASTLE MAGIC.

It's all in your mind.

{JIMI'S RECORD LABEL, WARNER BROS., REACHED A SETTLEMENT GIVING PPX AND ITS DISTRIBUTOR, CAPITOL RECORDS, THE RIGHTS TO JIMI'S NEXT ALBUM.}

CAPITOL RECORDS WERE PUSHING US FOR A NEW RECORD, so I got Buddy Miles on drums and Billy Cox on bass. We spent twelve to eighteen hours a day practicing this whole last week, straight ahead! We were just getting off, that's all. We'd say "rehearsing" just to make it sound official. And then we went to a little funky club and jammed down there to test it out and see how the air was. We're calling it the Band Of Gypsys, because that's what we are. That's what all musicians are. The whole world is their front porch.

Musically, we try to keep it together. That's why the personnel in groups changes all the time – because they're always searching for that certain little thing. The fact of calling it Gypsys means it could even expand on personnel and so forth. I might not even be there all the time. Buddy might not even be there all the time. But the core, the whole, the child will be there.

We're just going to be laying down what we see today. That's our theme. Not sad blues, blues today. We have one song called *Earth Blues*. It's all bottom. It's all rhythm. Buddy is getting all the voices together so they will become another instrument. We do a thing called *Them Changes*, too. Buddy wrote this one, and I'd like to have him sing it. And we do this one called *Message To Love*. Everybody's rappin' about love, so we'll put in our two cents' worth and see what it sounds like ...

WELL WORLD,
I SAID WE'RE TRAVELIN AT A SPEED
OF A REBORN MAN.
WE GOT A LOT OF LOVE TO GIVE,
YA BETTER COME ON IF YA CAN.
I'M TALKIN BOUT LOVE,
DON'T TRY TO RUN AWAY.
CHECK YOURSELF OUT BABY,
AND THEN COME WITH ME TODAY.

The background of our music is a spiritual blues thing. Now I want to bring it down to earth. I want to get back to the blues, because that's what I am. When music goes too far out and is in danger of becoming a technique, people always come back to basic honesty. That's why the blues and country & western music are at the foundations of our popular music.

The blues are easy to play, but not to feel. You've got to know much more than the mere technicalities of notes. You've got to know sounds and what goes between the notes. Most people believe that to be a good blues musician one has to suffer. I don't believe this. When I hear certain notes I feel real happy. I just like the sound of the blues. We used to say a thing like, if you don't have no blues with you, we'll make some to take home.

Blues is part of America. Blues will never die.

{To satisfy the PPX-Capitol settlement, the Band Of Gypsys recorded
their debut at the Fillmore East in New York.}

We went onstage New Year's Eve and New Year's Day at the
Fillmore East. That first set was really tight. It was scary. Buddy's
going to do most of the singing. I'd rather just play. In England they
made me sing, but Buddy has the right voice, so he's going to do the
singing from now on. Anyway, I can't do the screaming out and
hollering bit much longer. Music can make it for you, I know, but
I'm not quite as good as Bing Crosby.

{On January 28, 1970, the Band of Gypsys made their final appearance at
a benefit concert for the Vietnam Moratorium Committee at Madison
Square Garden. Jimi abruptly walked off stage in the middle
of the second number.}

It was just something where the head changes. Just going through
changes, I really couldn't tell you the truth. I was very tired.
Sometimes there's a lot of things that add up in your head about this
and that, and they hit you at a very peculiar time, which happened
to be at that peace rally. And there I am fighting the biggest war I've
ever fought in my life – inside, you know? And that wasn't the place
to do it, so I just unmasked appearances.

I figure that Madison Square Garden was like
the end of a big long fairy tale. It's the best
ending I could possibly have come up with.
It's like the end of a beginning.

NINE TO THE UNIVERSE

FORGET OF MY NAME.
REMEMBER IT ONLY AS A HANDSHAKE.
RIDE INSTEAD THE WAVES OF MY
INTERPRETURE, MUSIC, SOUND, HYPNOTIC,
IF YOU CHOOSE.

{AFTER THE ABORTED MADISON SQUARE GARDEN CONCERT, MIKE JEFFERY FIRED
BUDDY MILES AND TRIED TO REFORM THE ORIGINAL EXPERIENCE. JIMI HAD
OTHER PLANS.}

The Experience got into a cul-de-sac. We played for three years
and had reached the stage where we were just repeating ourselves.
Mitch will be playing with me. He's never been better than he is now.
Noel is definitely and confidently out.

It was my plan to change the bass player even back in the days after
the Experience when there was no band. It's nothing personal against
Noel. Billy Cox has a more solid style, which suits the new group
better. I'm not saying that anyone is better than the other, just that
today I want a more solid style. There's no telling how I'll feel
tomorrow.

{IN APRIL 1970, *STEPPING STONE*, WITH BILLY COX ON BASS AND BUDDY MILES
ON DRUMS, WAS RELEASED IN AMERICA AS A SINGLE. IT DIDN'T MAKE THE CHARTS
AND WAS SOON WITHDRAWN.}

I haven't had too many records out for a while. I wanted this out
before people forgot about me.

I'M A MAN, AT LEAST I TRY TO BE,
    BUT I'M LOOKING FOR THE OTHER HALF OF ME,
I'M LOOKIN' FOR THAT TRUE LOVE TO BE,
        MY ENDLESS SEARCH FOR MY TRUE DESTINY.

WELL, I TRY TRY NOT TO BE A FOOL.
    WELL, I TRY TRY LORD TO KEEP MY COOL, BABY,
TRY SO HARD TO KEEP IT TOGETHER.

I don't know how good it is. I can't tell anymore. Some of the copies out here have no bass on them. I had to go out somewhere and tell the guy to remix it, but he didn't. Sure it matters. I'd like a hit single. It's nice to have people hearing your songs all over the world on the radio.

I did some recording last year, but I flipped out after two days because much of the stuff was recorded in the gap between the time the Experience broke up and the Band of Gypsys. So that stuff's another age. I'm losing time with myself.

{APRIL ALSO SAW THE RELEASE OF THE *BAND OF GYPSYS* ALBUM RECORDED AT THE FILLMORE EAST. IT SPENT SIXTY-ONE WEEKS ON THE AMERICAN CHARTS AND REACHED A TOP POSITION OF #5.}

The only reason we put out *Band Of Gypsys* was that Capitol was pressing for an LP and we didn't have anything ready at the time. So they got that. I wasn't too satisfied with the album. If it had been up to me I would have never put it out. From a musician's point of view it was not a good recording, and I was out of tune on a few things. Not enough preparation went into it, and it came out a bit grizzly. We all felt shaky. There were some nice songs on the album, some nice ideas, particularly on side two.

{CONTINUING FINANCIAL PRESSURES FORCED JIMI TO ABANDON WORK ON HIS NEW
ALBUM AND AGREE TO YET ANOTHER TOUR OF AMERICA.}

I'm calling the tour "Cry Of Love" because that's what it's all about. One of the worst statements people are making is, "No man is an island." Every man is an island, and music is about the only way we can really communicate. It's a crusade, right?

A lot of people in America are looking for a leader in the music field. It'll take somebody like us to get it together. We'll be on a truth kick. We want to be completely honest and barefaced. We want to be respected after we're dead. Who doesn't want to be remembered in history? But regardless of whether it's going be us, the feeling is there, and that's what counts. If I die tomorrow, the feeling is there. Forget about brand names. We put across the music. The idea is to do it as strongly as possible, to work out a certain physical change.

The Beatles could do it. They could turn this world around or at least attempt to. The Beatles can be a positive force, and they could really get the people together. They've got power because they are performing for the masses. They should use their power. It might make them a little more uncomfortable in their position, but me, I don't care about my position. What I have to say I'm glad to say it. I'm trying to use my power. I could buy myself a house in Beverly Hills and retire, but I just want to go on trying to communicate. I am happy enough to spread my thoughts to others, so that's what I must do.

{THE "CRY OF LOVE" TOUR OPENED ON APRIL 25 AT THE LOS ANGELES FORUM. THREE DAYS AFTER AMERICANS CELEBRATED EARTH DAY 1970.}

"Listen, we're all in this mess together. *We're all livin', tryin' to grow, little children takin' steps here and there from home. And some have big dreams, and some of those get killed by all these bullshit old traditional schemes. So just try to dig the message. We already know hang-ups, we already know protest! Now we're going to try and give a few solutions. Let's see what kind of world we want to have. It's up to you all and it's up to us too, so let's get our feelings together.* Let's get our hearts together."

There's a whole lot of riots that are still going to happen in the States, and anywhere else for that matter. You sit glued to your TV and you're seeing the fantasy side of life. But the problems are still there. Out in the street, that's still there. I try to use my music as a machine to move these people to act, to get changes done. I know we can do it, that's not the problem. That's why we're suffering. That's why we party hard. That's why we suffer hard. The problem is, can you keep up?

*   *   *   *   *   *   *

I KNOW WHERE THE TROUBLE IS. A lot of it is laziness. On that side there there's going to have to be some people to get off their asses and try to get theirselves together, instead of sitting around smoke dens saying, "Yeah, man, this is groovy, yeah, protest, protest," and then come up with no kind of solution. Or if they come up with a solution they realize there might be a sacrifice they might have to make. Like some cat might have to give up his gig, which he calls "security," which is a slave thing.

YOU WORK HARD EVERY DAY, COME HOME EVERY NIGHT
    FEED THE CAT AND A DOG,
      TAKE A SMOKE AND EVERYTHING'S ALL RIGHT –
BUT THEN YOU SEE SHADOWS ON THE WALL,
      VOICES SCREAM FROM 1000 HALLS
    AND YOU KNOW IT'S COMING FROM
        ROUND THE CORNER.

THE YEARS PASS BY, AND NOW YOU'RE 82 –
    YOU THINK BACK ON YOUR LIFE
    AND IT WORRIES EVEN YOU
    AND YOU SAY TO YOURSELF –
      I AIN'T DID A THING
    AND YOU DRAG OUT YOUR TIME MACHINE
      AND MAKE IT BACK TO THE TIME
    WHEN YOU NEVER WENT
        AROUND THE CORNER.

We must watch out. Security, the thinking, the reaching for it, is the biggest drug, the worst drug that's happening today. Once you outlaw that feeling a whole lot of other things will start happening. That's the way I live now. I don't have a clear-cut plan. I love the uncertainties of the future. If you know beforehand what is going to happen then, to me, life doesn't make sense. There are, of course, certain things that I would like to do, and it's very possible that I will destroy myself in my attempt to achieve these things.

TODAY I BURN UNDER MY BRAIN'S CONSCIOUSNESS
  OF WHAT PROPELS ME OUT OF TROUBLE,
AT TIMES INTO TIME ITSELF,
   OUTSIDE INTO THE SPACE OF IT ALL.
 MY BODY CANNOT BREATHE THERE.
   WHAT IS MY MIND DOING THERE?
WHY IS MY SOUL SURPASSING CURIOUS EGO'S SECURITY ACT,
  GOING FAST AS THE SPEED OF THOUGHT,
THE FASTEST AND LONGEST FAR-REACHING THING WE KNOW?

As long as you're off your ass and on your feet some kind of way. Out of the bed and into the street, **blah-blah, woof-woof, crackle-crackle.** We can tap dance to that, can't we?

If you want to know the truth about it, the best thing to do is listen to the music. When there are vast changes in the way the world goes, it's usually something like art and music that change it. Music is going to change the world next time. **You see, music doesn't lie.**

I agree it can be misinterpreted, but it doesn't lie.

{On May 4, 1970, four students were shot dead by the National Guard during an anti–Vietnam War demonstration at Kent State University, Ohio.}

"THIS IS DEDICATED TO ALL THE SOLDIERS FIGHTIN' IN KENT STATE – ALL FOUR OF THEM! AND ALL THE SOLDIERS IN MADISON AND MILWAUKEE. OH YES, I ALMOST FORGOT, VIETNAM AND CAM-BOOH-DI-AAHH! SO MANY WARS GOIN' ON. WHAT A DRAG ALL THAT SHIT IS! NEXT THING YOU KNOW EVERY ONE OF THESE KIDS'LL BE COMPLETELY WIPED OUT BECAUSE OF SOME SHIT THAT OLD PEOPLE SAID! FREEDOM FOR US ALL!"

A lot of people want to be written down in war history, written down in money history. This is nothing but child's play for so-called grown-ups. Countries to me are just like little kids playing with different toys, and nobody can go out on the streets with this little boy, America's little boy. What a **DRAG** that America's guns have made the **CRACK** in the Liberty Bell their symbol! There's other ways you can settle things, there's other ways you can live.

{Because of the antiwar demonstrations, when Jimi played at Berkeley Community Center on May 30, the neighborhood was close to being put under martial law.}

"Hate to say it, but there's a lot of truth we have to face up to. The idea is solutions, but still we got dedications to all the soldiers in Chicago that are in jail, all the soldiers in New York, Florida, right here in Berkeley — especially the soldiers in Berkeley. *You know what soldiers I'm talking about. And dedicate it to other people that might be fightin' wars too, but within themselves, not facing up to realities. We're gonna play the American anthem the way it really is in the air in which you breathe every day, the way it really sounds. We're all in this mess together.*
We're gonna play OUR American anthem.*"*

The kids on the campus are shouting through a keyhole. They're not being individuals. In American riots you see these masochist kids. They go in there with no shelter, no anything. They get beat. Some of them will say, "We don't have nothin' else to live for anyway. This is our scene now."

You can see how desperate the whole case must be if a kid's going to go out there without protection and get his head busted open. But then you look over in Japan. The kids in Japan, they buy helmets and they got their little squadrons and they go in wedges, like this. They got all their stuff together. They've got their shields. They're wearing steel supports. You have to have all these things.

I'd like to see these American kids with helmets on and big Roman shields and then do their thing. Really together! If you're going to go in there, you might as well make it together. And you must put this in the book, because I'm tired of seeing Americans get their heads split open for no reason at all.

229

{THROUGH MAY, JUNE AND JULY 1970, THE "CRY OF LOVE" TOUR CRISS-CROSSED
AMERICA, PERFORMING IN MORE THAN THIRTY AMERICAN CITIES.}

*"I'd like to dedicate this show to the American Deserters Society.
So we'll try to help 'em out and do a song, the International Anthem,
bringin' all the soldiers back from Vietnam. Instead of them marching
down the street with big M-60s and big submarines and all this stuff on
their backs, how 'bout they march into town with big feedback guitars?*
Yeah, let's come on back from Vietnam there!"

America is inclined to bring out the rebel in me, and I'm not really
like that at all. I still love America, naturally, it has so much good in
it. But it has so much evil too. The way this country's being run you
can see the badness, you can see the evil, right in front of your face.

On the one side the people are like pelicans who all think the
same. They are striving for dead, useless things. Then we have the
American Revolution, fake love for the LIE people who sold their
faith. Quite naturally you say, "Make love, not war," but then you
come back to reality. There are some evil folks around and they want
you to be passive and weak and peaceful so they can overtake you like
jelly on bread. It's good to be passive and all this, but you have to
have something to back it up. You have to fight fire with fire.

Forget about the mass-love scene. It's not building understanding.
And I wish I could say this so strongly they'd sit up in their chairs,
because there's no such thing as love until truth and understanding
come about. In order to change the world you have to get your own
head together first.

{IN MAY 1970, AFTER A YEAR OF STRUGGLING TO BUILD ELECTRIC LADY STUDIOS, JIMI WAS FINALLY ABLE TO BEGIN RECORDING THERE.}

I have done great things with this place. It has the best equipment in the world. It is capable of recording on 32 tracks, which takes care of most things. There is one thing that I hate about studios usually, and that is the impersonality of them. They are cold and blank, and within a few minutes I lose all drive and inspiration.

Electric Lady is different. It has been built with great atmosphere. There are lots of cushions and pillows and thick carpets and soft lights. It's a very relaxed studio with every comfort, so it makes people feel they are recording at home. And you can have any kind of light combination you feel like. I think this is very important. I want it to be an oasis for all the rock and roll musicians in New York. Chuck Berry and Sly have been down there doing a few things, and I am working on a symphony production to be done there in the near future.

I'M ALSO WORKING ON MY OWN ALBUM, called *First Ray Of The New Rising Sun*. *The First Ray Of The New Rising Sun* is my new life. It will be about what we have seen, and will simplify it all to bridge the gap between teenagers and parents. It's going to be a double set again and have about twenty tracks on it. Some tracks are getting very long, but you see, our music doesn't pertain to one thing. You don't have to be singing about love all the time in order to give love.

I wrote a song called *Trashman,* which I'll explain. There's a physical change coming soon, and the world's going to go topsy-turvy. It's neither bad nor good – it's just true. Because humans forget that they're part of earth-matter too, they have bad vibrations floating around right now. For instance, you sometimes go into smoke dens and find that nobody is contributing to nothing. It's nothing but a big negative.

So there's going to be this big physical change where you can draw all negative energies that might be around out of people. And from that energy you will be able to talk for about thirty hours straight, talk about something right and true. I mean talk about something that has some kind of foundation. Everybody should play their own parts. Everybody should be actors in their own scripts. All of the script is coming from God in the first place. It's up to them to play out their parts.

Then we have *Valleys Of Neptune Arising*, and we have one called *Astro Man.* Talk about living in peace of mind, well, *Astro Man* will leave you in pieces! We have the theme from *The New Rising Sun*, this little bolero type of thing. It's kind of nice, but then it breaks down into a very simple pattern, asking this one question, *"Where are you coming from and where are you going to?"*

I think we're going to have this thing called *Horizon* or *Between Here And Horizon*, and that goes into certain things like *A Letter To The Room Full Of Mirrors.* That's more of a mental disarrangement. It's a song about when you get real high and all you can see is you, reflections of you here and there. Some of you have undoubtedly been through this at one time or another, in some kind of way or another.

Oh boy! I guess I'll try and get rid of that hang-up. Like they say, on a clear day you can see forever.

THERE ARE BASICALLY TWO KINDS OF MUSIC. The blues is a reflection of life, and then there is sunshine music, which may not have so much to say lyrically but has more meaning musically. It's more an easier type of thing with less worries and more meaning to it. I really don't want to get too heavy. I want to play sunshine music now. I have this saying that when things get too heavy, "Just call me helium, the lightest known gas to man!"

But music is always changing according to the attitude of the people. When the air is static, loud and aggressive, that's how the music gets. When the air starts getting peaceful and harmonic, that's how the music will get. So it's up to the people how it's going to be.

MUSIC GOES BY THE RULES OF THE PRESENT AIR.
LISTEN PASSIVELY AS MY GUITAR HOWLS
AND GRINDS AND UNWINDS AND DINES
UPON THE SPELLING OF YOUR NAME.

I'd like to get into more symphonic things, so the kids can respect the old musical traditions, the classics. I'd like to mix that in with so-called rock. But I have to get involved in my own kind of way, because I always want to respect my own judgments.

233

I don't plan to just go out there with a ninety-piece orchestra and play two and a half hours of classical music. I plan for both those things to be used without even knowing that it's rock and classical, with it being a whole other thing. It would be just like every step is, a mixture of the past and the future. When I finally get into it the whole world's going to know about it.

IT WOULD BE INCREDIBLE IF YOU COULD PRODUCE MUSIC so perfect that it would filter through you like rays and ultimately cure. I'm into this combination of music and color. It's an extra area of awareness.

I have plans that are unbelievable, but then wanting to be a guitar player seemed unbelievable at one time. I only regret that I didn't start singing and playing on my own much earlier. I also regret that I'm lazy. I used to write thousands of tunes, but I don't seem to get around to it now.

{On July 30, 1970, Jimi appeared at the "Rainbow Bridge Vibratory Color/Sound Experiment" on the Hawaiian island of Maui.}

When I was in Hawaii I saw a beautiful thing, a miracle. There were lots of rings around the moon, and the rings were all women's faces. I wish I could tell someone about it ...

BABY CHILD AS A MAN,
AS A LIVING GRAIN OF SAND,
SITTING ON THE EVER-CHANGING SHORE,
GREETING THE SUNRISE ...

PICKED UP UPON THE GYPSY WOMAN,
HAIR FLAMING NIGHT AS RAVENS
EVEN SLEEP ... RAINBOW CLOTH ...
TAMBOURINE COMPLEMENTING HER CHANT
AND CHOICE OF GRACES,
AND LOVE HER GOD.

I ACTUALLY LOOKED UPON HER
ON MY RIGHT ... COMING FORTH,
AND BABY CHILD THEN SECONDLY LOOKED
HIS LEFT TO EYE,
AND 11 OR 12 WOMEN, MEN
AND LITTLE ONES APPROACHED,
THEY CLAD IN THEIR MASTER'S WISH;
WHITE ROBES SWAYING TO BE BAPTIZED.

THESE TWO WORLDS CROSSED EACH OTHER
IN FRONT OF ME, WHEN AFTERWARDS ...
BABY CHILD SIPPED A HEARTFUL OF OCEAN,
SPAT OUT THE WASTE AND WALKED
UPON THE NEW DAY.

I see miracles every day now. I used to be aware of them maybe once or twice a week, but some are so drastic that I couldn't explain them to a person or I'd probably be locked up by this time. One of these days I'll finally release all that out, but I'm not going to say anything about it until a wide range of people see it. It's a universal thought; it's not a black and white thing, or a green and gold thing ...

People are frightened to find out the full power of the mind. At the moment, people use only a minute part of their minds, and there's so much more scope. At one time man could see right around the world with his third eye. That was something that's always been there. If we could only redevelop those old skills.

I think the way things are going right now, maturity, that's going to take time. But spirituality and things in the head, they're always there. I mean, it gets better and better all the time. I'm always having visions, and I know it's building up to something really major. It's out of what's directing me. What I was here in the first place to do.

{JIMI CONTINUED RECORDING AT ELECTRIC LADY STUDIOS THROUGHOUT AUGUST. THE STUDIO WAS OFFICIALLY OPENED ON AUGUST 26.}

New York is killing me at the moment. It's positively claustrophobic! Things go so fast you might as well step on a roller coaster each time you move outside your door. One day I saw a soldier in the street and said, "Hey, how are you?" He just stared at me and said, "Hey, man, are you for real?" He was bringing himself down because he was so full of hate.

I BELIEVE YOU HAVE TO LIVE AND LIVE AGAIN until you have got all the evil and hatred out of your soul. Your body is as unimportant as one fish in the sea compared with your soul. But there are still some hardheads who don't give themselves a chance to develop in the brain, or to let the soul develop or the emotions. You've got to gentle these people along for a while until they are clued in on the scene. With enough love and faith, they can find themselves again.

There's no bad people or good people; it's actually all lost and found. That's what it all boils down to. There's a lot of lost people around, and there are a few chosen people that are here to help get these people out of this certain sleepiness that they are in. There's going to be sacrifices. You have to go down into a really bad scene before you can come up with light again. It's like death and rebirth. After you've gone through all of the hell of dying, you've got to find out and face the facts to start a nationwide rebirth.

The whole past is going towards a higher way of thinking. There'll be a day when houses will be made of diamonds and emeralds. Bullets'll be fairy tales. There'll be a renaissance from bad to completely clear and pure and good – from lost to found.

TRUMPETS AND VIOLINS I CAN HEAR IN THE DISTANCE
 I THINK THEY'RE CALLING OUR NAMES.
MAYBE NOW, YOU CAN'T HEAR THEM, BUT YOU WILL
IF YOU JUST TAKE HOLD OF MY HAND.

I attribute my success to God. It all comes from God. I go by message, and I'm really a messenger of God. My name is nothing but a distraction. Already this idea of living today is magic. I'm working on music to be completely, utterly a magical science, where it's all pure positive. The more doubts and negatives you knock out of anything, the heavier it gets and the clearer it gets, and the deeper it gets into whoever's around it. It's contagious. Bach and all those cats, they went in there, and they caught a whole lot of hell.

The deeper you get into it, the more sacrifices you have to make. It means I'm going to have to strip myself of my identity, because this isn't my only identity. Really I'm just an actor. The only difference between me and those cats in Hollywood is that I write my own script. Someone is going to have to go back to his childhood and think about what they really felt, really wanted before the fingerprints of their fathers and mothers got a hold of them, or before the smudges of school or progress ...

{ON AUGUST 30, 1970, JIMI RETURNED TO GREAT BRITAIN TO PLAY AT THE ISLE OF WIGHT FESTIVAL, HIS FIRST APPEARANCE IN ENGLAND IN ONE AND A HALF YEARS.}

It's nice to be back. I've been away from this country and Europe for such a long time. But the band has been committed to so many tours and college gigs in the States that it was utterly impossible for us to come over. Believe me, we wanted to! We'd mention that we'd like to come back to Britain to play, but our business people would tell us, "You're nothing over there in Britain at the moment. Besides, you've got this booking in Boston ..."

We received a lot of STATIC in New York, a lot of aggravation in New York. So I've been doing like Yogi Bear, I've been hibernating. I just tried to do the gigs and stay quiet for a while. I've been going through certain changes. I guess it's something else for people to talk about.

While I was doing my vanishing act in the States, I got this feeling that I was completely blown out of England. I thought maybe they didn't want me anymore, because they had a nice set of bands. Maybe they were saying, "Oh, we've had Hendrix, yeah, he was okay." I really didn't think we'd have any drawing power.

I'm so very nervous about the Isle of Wight, I can't believe it. I really hate waiting around like this. I think it would be better if I'd come and mingled, took a sleeping bag with me and mixed with the crowds to identify with it all. It would be so much better than all this, but there are the usual problems. If I do things like that the people keep coming up to me saying, "Look, it's him," and, "C'mon, c'mon" and all that, prodding me.

I'm just a little bit worried now because I sound a teeny bit like a frog. Last night we were playing so loud that I was shouting on my tiptoes. I felt like my kneecaps were up in my chest nearly. I get kind of tense before a show. I like to be left alone to think. I have to think myself into my act. I can't just turn on.

My road manager tries to keep the dressing room free from people, and if people come in I find a corner somewhere else. So right now I just feel kind of nervous, but I think it will be all right, because now we're going to go on and do our little gig. Mitch will be playing drums and Billy will be playing bass and I'll be playing GUITAR! **You know, instead of up there screaming.**

Most of the time we play a whole vacuum, I mean a wall of sound, a wall of feeling. That's what we try to get across, you know what I mean? Shhheeeooo! We haven't been to sleep for two days. I'm tired, and I don't have much time.

The Isle of Wight might be the last or second to the last before I form my new big band. If the kids really enjoy it, then I might carry on a little longer. But I will only carry on that way if I am useful. You have got to have a purpose in life. But I'm not here to talk, I'm here to play. I want to show them all over again what it's all about.

I'm happy. It's going to be good.

"Yeah! Thank you very much for showin', man.
You're all very beautiful and outasight.
And thanks for waiting. It has been a long time, hasn't it …
Oh yes, somebody wants the people in the front row to sit down.
I think it's probably from the hills.
Don't forget you can't fly off the top of those hills.

Don't forget that."

Is the Isle of Wight the last of the big festivals?

> I don't know why they're always trying to kill the festivals.
> The Isle of Wight was great. It's a fantastic place to have a
> show because it brings the kids together from not only the
> British Isles but also the whole of the Continent.

There were problems with some of the crowd.

> You're going to get that with five hundred thousand
> people. That's way larger than the average city, and every
> city in the world always has a gang, the so-called outcasts.
> So you're going to have gate-crashers, you're going to have
> the other side of everything.

People were demanding that the music be free.

> Well, they learned that from the papers. They didn't do all
> that kind of mess with Monterey. Sometimes I feel we
> should do a free concert. I see the prices that the kids pay
> to see us, and it's just ridiculous.

What is the reason for the new, subdued Jimi Hendrix?

> I felt maybe too many people were coming to see me and
> not enough to listen to me. My nature changed as well.
> I just hid for a bit, and now I'm emerging as me. I suppose
> I'm growing up a bit. I feel as though I get little sparks of
> maturity every now and then.

Do you ever see yourself settling down?

> I couldn't even think of a place where I'd like to live for the rest of my life, but I'd like to settle someplace eventually. Sometimes I am all alone and I say, "What are you doing here dressed up in satin shirts and pants?" I've got this feeling to have a proper home. I like the idea of getting married, just someone who I could love, though one can never tell if the time is right. With music there's no time for anything else. I'm already married to my music.

So marriage is not an option?

> Marriage is a bit risky now. I'd really hate to get hurt. That would completely blow my mind. But I must admit I'd like to meet a quiet little girl now, probably one from the country, someone who doesn't know anything about me and my reputation. One day I want to become a parent. Now that is what the world is all about. Having kids. Like planting flowers.

How do you relax?

> I daydream, maybe paint landscapes, read a little. I've always loved painting. In fact it was my first love when I was a child. I used to paint a picture of, say, a really pretty mountain, then write about four lines of poetry about it. I don't hardly get a chance to paint now.

What plans do you have now?

> I'd like to see as many places as I can and play in as many

atmospheres as I can. Your home isn't America, it's the Earth. I am planning a major world tour, either before or just after Christmas. I want to go to Japan and Australia. We also want to come back to England and do one big concert at each of the major cities. Jimi Hendrix at the Oval! I'd like to do Stonehenge, for the vibes. In fact, I want the group to work all over the place. I want to turn the world on. Music and sound waves are cosmic when they're flying from one side to another.

Any personal ambitions?

I'd like to have my own country, an oasis for the gypsy-minded people. My goal is to erase all boundaries from the world. I'd like to take part in changing reality. You have to set some heavy goals to keep yourself going. As long as I know there are people out there who aren't fully together, I can't withdraw to lesser goals.

Do you have enough money to live comfortably?

Ah, I don't think so. Because I want to wake up in the morning and just roll out of my bed into an indoor swimming pool and then swim to the breakfast table, come up for air and maybe get a drink of orange juice, and then swim into the bathroom and, you know ... have a shave.

You want to live luxuriously?

Is that luxurious? No! I was thinking about a tent, maybe, overhanging a mountain stream.

{THE CRY OF LOVE BAND PLAYED SIX MORE CONCERTS IN EUROPE, DURING WHICH
BILLY COX BECAME SERIOUSLY ILL WHEN LSD WAS SLIPPED INTO SOMETHING HE
WAS DRINKING. THE LAST SHOW WAS ON SEPTEMBER 6, 1970, AT THE VIOLENCE-
BESOTTED ISLE OF FEHMARN LOVE AND PEACE FESTIVAL IN GERMANY.}

Billy Cox has split, so I don't know what to do next. I don't know
what my music will be like. It's really hard to know what people want
around here sometimes. I'm going to just go on and do what I feel,
but I can't feel anything right now because there's a few things that's
just happened. So I just have to lay back and think about it all. It's
got to be quiet for a while.

I'm so tired of everything. I lose myself, I can't play anymore. I've
been working very hard for three years. I sacrifice part of my soul
every time I play. Certain things recharge me in an instant. I might
get worn out in an instant too. It all depends.

IT WASN'T TOO LONG AGO,
BUT IT FEELS LIKE YEARS AGO SINCE
I FELT THE WARM HELLO OF THE SUN.
LATELY THINGS SEEM A LITTLE COLDER,
THE WIND, IT SEEMS TO GET A LITTLE BOLDER,
THE EAGLE FLYING,
NOW IT'S ON THE RUN — BUT THEN AGAIN
IT'S ALL IN MY MIND.

Direction is the hardest thing for me to find now. I can't even try and think how this life has affected me. Somehow I must have changed, but I can't know how. That's the problem. I've turned full circle. I'm right back where I started. I've given this era of music everything, but I still sound the same and I can't think of anything new to add to it in its present state. Sometimes I can't stand to hear myself because it sounds like everyone else, and I don't want to be in that rat race.

The trouble is that people won't let me change. I tried a couple of years back, but it didn't work then either. You're still supposed to entertain, no matter what's happening to you as a musician. I wrote *Foxy Lady* so long ago by now she's going to have three kids. We'll dedicate it to her children, because she's worn out with it.

PURPLE HAZE – BEYOND INSANE.
IS IT PLEASURE OR IS IT PAIN?
DOWN ON THE CEILING
LOOKING UP AT THE BED,
SEE MY BODY PAINTED
BLUE AND RED.

I still can't figure out what directions my writing is going at the moment, but it'll find a way. All I write is what I feel, that's all. And I don't really round it off too good. It's almost naked. The words are so bland that nobody can get into them, and when we play – flip around and flash around – people just see what their eyes see, and forget about their ears.

I'm trying to do too many things at the same time, which is my nature. I just hate to be in one corner. I hate to be put as only a guitar player or only a songwriter or only a tap dancer! I like to move around. I've got to try something else. I'd like to get something together, like with Handel and Bach and Muddy Waters and flamenco – that type of thing. If I could get that sound, if I could get that sound, I'd be happy.

I think I'm a better guitarist than I was, but I never have been really good. Every year, like my writing, it slips further and further away. The music I might hear I can't get on the guitar. It's a thing of just laying around daydreaming or something. You're hearing all this music, and you just can't get it on the guitar.

As a matter of fact, if you pick up your guitar and try to play, it spoils the whole thing. I think of tunes, I think of riffs. I can hum them. Then there's another melody comes into my head and then a bass melody and then another one. On guitar, I just can't get them out. I can't play guitar well enough to get all this music together.

I want to be a good writer, and I'd like to be a good guitar player. I've learned a lot, but I've got to learn more about music because there's a lot in this hair of mine that's got to get out. There's so many songs I wrote that we haven't done yet, that we'll probably never do.

I WON'T BE DOING MANY LIVE GIGS because I'm going to develop the sound and then put a film out with it. In five years, I want to write some plays and some books. I want to write mythology stories set to music, based on a planetary thing and my imagination. It wouldn't be like classical music, but I'd use strings and harps, with extreme and opposite musical textures, even greater contrasts than Holst's *Planets*.

Then I would like to write a story for the stage and compose the music for it. Take Greek mythology, for example, or your old stories about the Vikings and Asgard. I'd like to present that on stage with lights and lots of sound. Or perhaps a space war between Neptune and Uranus.

*   *   *   *   *

MY INITIAL SUCCESS was a step in the right direction, but it was only a step. Now I plan to get into many other things. I'd like to take a six-month break and go to a school of music. I want to learn to read music, be a model student and study and think. I'm tired of trying to write stuff down and finding I can't. I want a big band. I don't mean three harps and fourteen violins, I mean a big band full of competent musicians that I can conduct and write for.

I want to be part of a big new musical expansion. That's why I have to find a new outlet for my music. We are going to stand still for a while and gather everything we've learned musically in the last 30 years, and we are going to blend all the ideas that worked into a new form of classical music. It's going to be something that will open up a new sense in people's minds.

I dig Strauss and Wagner, those cats are good, and I think that they are going to form the background of my music. Floating in the sky above it will be the blues – I've still got plenty of blues – and then there will be *western sky music* and *sweet opium music* (you'll have to bring your own opium!), and these will be mixed together to form one. And with this music we will paint pictures of earth and space, so that the listener can be taken somewhere. You have to give people something to dream on.

WHERE IS HE COMING FROM?
FROM HEAVEN WHERE A MILLION WORLDS ARE ONE
WHERE IS HE GOING TO? HE'S GOING TO MAKE
CONTACT WITH THE LIVING AND THE DEAD.

I T SEEMS TO ME LIKE MUSIC GOES IN A BIG CYCLE. The circle is completed and I'm starting back already. My goal is to be one with the music. I just dedicate my whole life to this art. You have to forget about what other people say, when you're supposed to die, or when you're supposed to be living. You have to forget about all these things. You have to go on and be crazy.

Craziness is like heaven. Once you reach that point where you don't give a damn what everybody else is saying, you're going towards heaven. The more you get into it, they're going to say, "Damn, that cat's really flipped out. Oh, he's gone now." That's what they call craziness. But if you're producing and creating, you're getting closer to your own heaven.

When the last American tour finished I just wanted to go away and forget everything. I just wanted to record and see if I could write something. Then I started thinking. Thinking about the future. Thinking that this era of music sparked off by the Beatles has come to an end. Something new has got to come, and Jimi Hendrix will be there.

The moment I feel that I don't have anything more to give musically, that's when I won't be found on this planet, unless I have a wife and children, because if I don't have anything to communicate through my music, then there is nothing for me to live for. I'm not sure I will live to be twenty-eight years old, but then again, so many beautiful things have happened to me in the last three years. The world owes me nothing.

When people fear death, it's a complete case of insecurity. Your body is only a physical vehicle to carry you from one place to another without getting into a lot of trouble. So you have this body tossed upon you that you have to carry around and cherish and protect and so forth, but even that body exhausts itself. The idea is to get your own self together, see if you can get ready for the next world, because there is one. Hope you can dig it.

People still mourn when people die. That's self-sympathy. All human beings are selfish to a certain extent, and that's why people get so sad when someone dies. They haven't finished using him. The person who is dead ain't crying. Sadness is for when a baby is born into this heavy world, and joy should be exhibited at someone's death because they are going on to something more permanent and infinitely better.

I tell you, when I die I'm going to have a jam session. I want people to go wild and freak out. And knowing me, I'll probably get busted at my own funeral. The music will be played loud and it will be our music. I won't have any Beatles songs, but I'll have a few of Eddie Cochran's things and a whole lot of blues. Roland Kirk will be there, and I'll try and get Miles Davis along if he feels like making it. For that it's almost worth dying. Just for the funeral.

It's funny the way people love the dead. You have to die before they think you are worth anything. Once you are dead, you are made for life.

When I die, just keep on playing the records.

THE STORY OF LIFE
IS QUICKER THAN
THE WINK OF AN EYE

THE STORY OF LOVE
IS HELLO AND GOOD-BYE

UNTIL WE MEET AGAIN

London, 18th September: Jimi Hendrix, the American rock star whose passionate, intense guitar playing stirred millions, died here today of unknown causes. He was 27 years old.

*   *   *   *   *   *   *

Narrative composition and Introduction: PETER NEAL
Authentication and compilation of source material: MICHAEL FAIRCHILD
Design and art direction: DAVID COSTA, Wherefore Art?
(with thanks to NICKY PAGE)
Project coordination: KEITH ROBINSON
Illustrations: BILL SIENKIEWICZ
Consultant: RAY RAE GOLDMAN
Final edit: ROSS FIRESTONE
Business administration: MARCO MERCIECA (Tri-Mer Services)
Associate Producer: MICHAEL LEMESRE
Legal Counsel: KIRK HALLAM

PRODUCED BY ALAN DOUGLAS
WITH SPECIAL THANKS TO SANDY LIEBERSON AND JOHN MASOURI
FOR HELPING TO FREE THIS BOOK FROM CAPTIVITY

✻   ✻   ✻   ✻   ✻   ✻   ✻

PICTURE ACKNOWLEDGMENTS

COVER AND TITLE PAGE:
Jimmy at 3 by DELORES HAMM HALL {courtesy Leon Hendrix Collection}
Jimi at 25 by GERED MANKOWITZ {©2013 Bowstir Ltd/mankowitz.com}

PHOTO REFERENCE FOR ILLUSTRATIONS:
p6 ©Joel Axelrad/Cache Agency
p12 photographer Delores Hamm Hall {courtesy Leon Hendrix Collection}
p33 courtesy Leon Hendrix Collection
p34 original photo by William *PoPsie* Randolph
p50 K&K Ulf Kruger OHG/Redferns/Getty Images
p86 Michael Ochs Archive/Getty Images
p104 Express/Hulton Archive/Getty Images
p134 David Redfern/Redferns/Getty Images
p166 ©Joel Axelrad/Cache Agency
p196 Elliot Landy/Redferns/Premium Archive/Getty Images
p213 Reg Innell/Toronto Star
p220 John Titchen, Honolulu
p253 Central Press/Hulton Archive/Getty Images
p255 Nona Hatay

For information concerning the sources used in this book, please go to **www.startingatzero.net**

* * * * * * *